BANKRUPTCY, HOW TO SURVIVE AND PROSPER

A personal journey through bankruptcy

LEIGHANN RYAN

BookSurge Publishing

ISBN: 1-4392-5334-X
ISBN-13: 9781439253342

Visit www.booksurge.com to order additional copies.

*For the man who makes everyday
of my life a special day,
my husband*

TABLE OF CONTENTS

INTRODUCTION

It has been said that humans can live thirty days without food, ten days without water, eight minutes without oxygen but not a minute without hope. *Bankruptcy, How to Survive and Prosper* was written to help the millions of people searching for hope and encouragement. When you file for bankruptcy, know that you are on your way up and not down. This book will demystify bankruptcy. There is so much misinformation out there about bankruptcy and the stigma it carries. Many financial experts will tell you that bankruptcy is one of the worst mistakes you can make. I am not a financial guru, just an ordinary, everywoman who has experienced one and is willing to tell the truth about it. The most important truth I discovered is that once you file, the healing begins. The bankruptcy was the easy part; the hard part was all the pain and despair leading up to it.

There are many myths that unfortunately scare people from considering bankruptcy. You may hear that bankruptcy is expensive, it is not. A Chapter 7 bankruptcy will cost several hundred dollars, a pittance really when you think of what you get in return, your life back. A Chapter 13 can cost several thousand dollars, but the majority of this cost, about ninety percent is paid for out of your monthly payments to the trustee, and will be pennies on the dollar of the amount you owe to the credit card companies.

Many fear that they will lose all their possessions. That is false, most likely you will lose very little in a Chapter 7 unless you have huge amounts of equity or you own the possession free and clear. In a Chapter 13, you will most likely get to keep everything. We did. Another myth is that you will have no control over your finances. Not true either. Probably the biggest myth of all is that everyone will know. Unless you are a famous person, chances are the only people who will know are your lawyer, the trustee and your mail person when they deliver mail from the bankruptcy court. To this day nobody in our family knows we have had a bankruptcy. Also, if you have a loan that is not included in your bankruptcy petition, the holder of that loan would be notified because the law mandates that everyone you owe money to must be notified whether they are included in the bankruptcy or not. For instance, your mortgage lender would be advised that you have filed a bankruptcy even though your house loan is not part of the bankruptcy and you will still be making your payment directly to the lender.

The sheer numbers are staggering. Every thirty seconds in the United States, someone files for bankruptcy. The United Kingdom sees 430 Great Britains a day go bankrupt. In Canada, 100, 000 people a year seek bankruptcy protection. The good news? You are so not alone.

You can read the how-to books on the nuts and bolts but what about the emotional toll and psychological impact? You have probably heard that bankruptcy ranks right up there with loss of a job, divorce and serious illness as one of life's biggest crisis. I would comb through the books in the library and bookstore, pulling them down, one by one, scanning the table of contents to see if there was any information to help deal with the pain. How obvious it should be that a financial crisis takes an enormous toll on our feelings and psyche, why wasn't there information available on how to deal with the emotional toll?

All my life when I needed information, it could always be found in a book, but not this time. I decided to write one myself, to help the many people going through the same situation. This is not about the legalities of bankruptcy, it is about the personal impact on our hearts and minds. Is there a protocol on how to behave or feel, should I feel shame, guilt, embarrassment, dare I say relief, is that all right or does it imply I got away with something? So many questions, so few answers.

I remember the feelings of utter worthlessness. For the first time in my life I actually understood how some people could be driven to commit suicide, not that I ever contemplated it. But with pure despair becoming my new best friend, it was apparent to me how some people feeling this same pain could feel that suicide would be the best way out for them. In my research, one recurring theme heard from others was that they just wished that they could go to sleep and never wake up. And the really frightening thing was that I had actually had the same thought.

Looking back, it is plain to see that it was not the bankruptcy that caused the pain, it was the events leading up to it. Once you file, life turns around dramatically, for the better. This is when the healing begins.

If you must go through a life altering situation, you would do well to take this experience and use it to turn your life around and prosper more than you could ever imagine. You can come out far better off than if you never had to join that club in the first place. You can come to see it as a blessing in your life. Can this be true? Could bankruptcy be the proverbial cloud with a silver lining?

Consider this. It is far better to spend some time in "time out". Look at the big picture. You spend a relatively short period of time, in addition to far less pain. You can then be set up for life, filled with power and free from fear. Your experience and survival profoundly ups the chance of you living out your life with financial peace and security, a concept that you could scarcely imagine in the clutches of a financial meltdown, bent and crushed under unmanageable debt.

What do we have in common with Bear Stearns, the United States' fifth largest investment house? According to an article in the Morning Journal on April 4, 2008, Bear Stearns was on the verge of declaring bankruptcy protection because nervous investors were demanding to be paid. The only difference between Bear Stearns and us is that we didn't have the Federal Reserve Chairman and the Bush Administration rescuing us. A default by Bear Stearns, given the exceptional pressures on the global economy and financial system, would cause damage severe and difficult to contain. Both Ben Bernanke and the Bush Administration agreed that the move was necessary to protect our economy.

Bear Stearns was purchased by JP Morgan Chase and Co. with assistance from the Federal government in the form of a loan backed by $30 million of Bear Stearns assets. JP Morgan also agreed to absorb the first $1 billion of losses if the value of the assets declined, but taxpayers are at risk for the remaining $29 billion.

Lawmakers questioned Ben Bernanke and the Bush Administration as to why the government was helping Wall Street but not Main Street. The answer was that the consequences to the United States economy and financial system would have been far more serious had the government allowed the nations' fifth largest investment house to go under.

Maybe they should tell that to Joe and Janice Pimentel of Atwater, California. Underneath the article about the bailout of Bear Stearns was an article about farm communities suffering a high rate of foreclosures. There was a picture of a man and woman, Joe and Janice, standing in front of a farm they had just lost in foreclosure. No bail out there. Just a hard working couple, trying to make a living, and losing.

Next to the article about Joe and Janice and under the article about the Bear Stearns bailout, there was an article on ATA Airlines filing for bankruptcy. It seems that ATA Airlines shut down operations and stranded thousands of travelers when an unexpected loss of key charter flights and soaring fuel costs forced the carrier into bankruptcy, for the second time in three years. The company's 2,200 employees were told, poof, your jobs are gone. Many passengers learned of the collapse at the ticket counters as they waited in line to get checked in to board their scheduled flight. Advisories had been posted at the counters advising passengers holding a ticket on ATA were not going anywhere today. All those passengers who thought they were going on that vacation or to that important business meeting got a rude surprise that day.

What is my point? So many good people are fighting the good fight and still losing. If big business can get into financial difficulties and get absolution, why should we feel bad because we also have financial difficulty, just on a smaller scale. It is doubtful Bear Stearns is going around hanging its' head in shame, and neither should we be. If a conglomerate like Bear Stearns, with all its' resources and brain power, can get into a financially difficult situation, and actually get bailed out for the good of the economy, why am I feeling so bad?

Really good question, the answer is I shouldn't and neither should you. Why should the average, little person feel that we have committed some grievous act? Some businesses actually use bankruptcy as a business model. When big business goes bankrupt, oh well, business as usual. They usually regroup and reopen some time down the road. What about all the chaos and job loss they leave in their wake? Business as usual.

Besides ATA Airlines, here is a partial list of other well known bankrupt businesses.

Kmart

Federated Department Stores

Montgomery Ward

Macy (R.H.) & Co., Inc.

Allied Stores Corp

Southland Corp

Ames Department Stores (twice)

The Circle K Corp

Carter Hawley Hale Stores

Revco D.S. Inc.

Home Interiors

Penn Central

W.T. Grant

Vera Sun Energy

Lehman Brothers

Circuit City

Archway Cooky

Lennox China

Linens and Things

Land America

Bally Total Fitness

Mervyn's

Sharper Image

Bombay

Pilgrim Pride

K.B. Toys

Boscov's

Tweeter

CompUSA

Steve and Barry's
Levitz Furniture
Polaroid
Champion Air
Aladdin Gaming
Aloha Airlines
Ameridebt
Baldwin Piano and Organ
Ben Franklin Retail Stores
Bethlehem Steel Corp.
Bugle Boy Industries
Burlington Industries
Carolco Pictures, Inc.
Chiquita Brands International
Clothestime Stores, Inc.
Color Tile, Inc.
Continental Airlines (twice)
Converse, Inc.
Dairy Mart Convenience Stores, Inc.
Death Row Records
Delphi Corporation
Delta Airlines, Inc.
Dow Corning Corp.
Eastern Airlines
Easyriders, Inc.
Fitzgeralds Gaming Corp
Fredericks of Hollywood
Fruit of the Loom, Inc.
G. Heileman Brewing Co, Inc.

Gadzooks, Inc.

Garden Botanika, Inc.

Greyhound Lines, Inc.

Hawaiian Airlines, Inc.

Houlihans Restaurants, Inc.

Huffy Corp

L.A. Gear, Inc.

Loehmann's, Inc.

Loews Cineplex Entertainment, Inc.

London Fog Group, Inc.

Maidenform, Inc.

Mars Music, Inc.

Marvel Entertainment Group

Midway Airlines Corp.

Mortgage Lenders Network USA, Inc.

Napster, Inc.

Northwest Airlines

Onieda Ltd.

Orion Pictures Corp

Owens Corning Corp

Pan Am Corp

Planet Hollywood International, Inc.

Polaroid Corp

Purina Mills, Inc.

Quebecor World (USA)

Rand McNally & Company

Regal Cinemas, Inc.

Resorts International, Inc.

Roadhouse Grill, Inc.

Ronco Corp

Schwinn/GT Corp

SevenUp/RC Bottling Company

Silicon Graphics, Inc.

Singer Company

Sizzler International

Smith Corona Corp.

Spiegle, Inc.

Texaco

The Roman Catholic Archdiocese of Portland, Oregon

Top-Flight Golf Company

TWA Airlines

United Artists Theatre Company

US Airways, Inc.

United Petroleum Corp

Vanguard Airlines, Inc.

Vlasic Foods International, Inc.

Western Union Corp

Winn-Dixie Stores, Inc.

WorldCom., Inc.

Zenith Electronics Corporation

WHO SHOULD READ THIS BOOK

While the millions of people facing bankruptcy today will benefit greatly by this book, they are not the only ones. Anyone who has ever had debt will find the information relevant and eye-opening.

This book is especially a must-read for anyone with credit card debt. Most people will go through their whole life never realizing the debilitating blow to their life caused by debt. The devastating toll exacted by debt is almost impossible to calculate. How can we even put a price on the worry and despair that becomes our new best friend when we are caught in the trap of credit card debt?

This book will serve as a cautionary tale for anyone who has or ever will have credit extended to them, which is pretty much everyone.

.

HOW TO READ THIS BOOK

The Rich, The Famous, The Everyperson reveals the names of many prominent people who have had a bankruptcy, people like Walt Disney, Henry Ford and Abraham Lincoln. It will also share three personal stories from ordinary people about their experience with bankruptcy.

A History of Bankruptcy reveals that bankruptcy has been around for hundreds of years and that there is indeed "nothing new under the sun". When put in a historical framework, it is far easier to put into proper perspective.

A Funny Thing Happened On The Way To Bankruptcy outlines my personal journey. It is an honest account, filled with humor and pathos. Many readers will instantly recognize themselves and their story within mine, and realize how very common their situation is. People love to read about others in the same boat that they are.

That Pesky Morality Question dissects just where morality fits into bankruptcy. It will show that morality can be highly subjective. The moral of the morality question is that it is, or should be, a non-issue.

Be Afraid, Be Very Afraid is about debt collectors, very dangerous people. The author shares personal horror stories and experiences she has had. Debt collectors can take your bad situation and make it worse than it was in the first place. Tips and advice are offered in dealing with them.

Debt Management, Debt Settlement, Debt Consolidation and Judgments will blow the lid off the players in this cottage industry set up to "help" the debt ridden consumer. The only people being "helped" however are the "counselors" (read salespeople). The dreaded judgment is explained and why you don't want one.

Why Plastic Is Hazardous To Your Wealth will address the true cost of debt and it is staggering. When we use plastic we greatly diminish our capacity to achieve prosperity in our life and obtain financial freedom.

Why Bankruptcy examines the choice between bankruptcy and alternative solutions. However solutions may be a misnomer, the consequences of not seeking bankruptcy protection are usually not very much of a solution.

How To Prosper After Bankruptcy offers both a financial philosophy and practical tips on how to achieve wealth after a bankruptcy. Prosperity is not only possible in spite of a bankruptcy but often because of a bankruptcy. Bankruptcy can be a catalyst to achieving wealth that you never could have achieved without the benefit of the knowledge you have gained through bankruptcy.

Getting Your Life And Future Back celebrates your second chance in life. The question is, what will you do with your second chance?

CHAPTER ONE

THE RICH, THE FAMOUS, THE EVERYPERSON

Sometimes we feel like we are alone in the world with our problem and nobody could possibly understand the stress and drama we live with everyday struggling with our financial ball-juggling. When you realize bankruptcy is a universally common phenomenon, going back hundreds of years, you'll find you are in pretty good company. Henry Ford filed bankruptcy five times before he found success and forever changed the world. If Henry Ford can rebound and go on to massive success, so can you and I. Walt Disney also had a bankruptcy as did Abraham Lincoln (twice). The following are some more names you may have heard of who also had a bankruptcy in their life.

Benedict Arnold

John James Audubon

P.T. Barnun

John Barrymore

Lionel Bart

Kim Basinger

Frank Baum

Barbara Bel Geddes

Melvin Belli

George Best

John Wayne Bobbitt

Peter Bogdanovich

Bjorn Borg

Lorraine Bracco
Toni Braxton
Lenny Bruce
Buffalo Bill
Gary Burghoff
Anita Bryant
Tia Carrere
Nell Carter
Miguel de Cervantes
Natalie Cole
Gary Coleman
John Connally
Francis Ford Coppola
Cathy Lee Crosby
Aleister Crowley
David Crosby
Vic Damone
Dorothy Dandridge
Daniel Defoe
Dino De Laurentis
John DeLorean
Clarissa Dickson Wright
Jim Dooley
Henry Dunant
William C. Durant
Eddy "The Eagle" Edwards
Chris Eubank
Freddy Fender
Stephin Fetchit

Eddie Fisher
Mick Fleetwood
Heidi Fleiss
William Fox
Red Foxx
Zsa Zsa Gabor
Leif Garrett
Marvin Gaye
Andy Gibb
Charles Goodyear
Ulysses S. Grant
Archie Griffin
Paulo Gucci
Bob Guccione
Johannes Gutenberg
Tony Gwynn
Merle Haggard
Corey Haim
Frans Hals
Dorothy Hamill
M.C. Hammer
George Frideric Handel
Richard Harris
Issac Hayes
Margaux Hemingway
Sherman Hensley
Milton Snavely Hershey
Perez Hilton
Nelson Bunker Hunt

Ron Isley
LaToya Jackson
Don Johnson
Janice-Marie Johnson
Al Jolson
George Jones
Grace Jones
Chaka Kahn
Charles Keating
Buster Keaton
Bernard Kerik
Margot Kidder
Larry King
Suge Knight
Lorenzo Lamas
Cyndi Lauper
Jerry Lee Lewis
Meat Loaf
Lisa "Left Eye" Lopes
Joe Louis
Jackie Mason
George McGovern
William McKinley
Marvin Mitchelson
Melba Moore
Lorrie Morgan
John Nash
Willie Nelson
Wayne Newton

Ted Nugent
Gaylord Perry
Thomas Paine
Tom Petty
Susan Powter
Randy Quaid
Lynn Redgrave
Rembrandt
Tommy Rettig
Burt Reynolds
Mickey Rooney
Oskar Schindler
Anna Nicole Smith
Lynn Spears
Lawrence Taylor
Mark Twain
Mike Tyson
Johnny Unitas
Oscar Wilde
Ray Winstone
Tammy Wynette
Florrenz Ziegfeld

Lest I be accused of urging anybody with debt to rush out and file bankruptcy, chances are if you are reading this, you don't need any urging, just some plain honest talk about what bankruptcy is really like. If your debt is manageable you surely should pay it. If you can conceivably pay off your debts without sacrificing your children's college fund, your retirement, your home, food on the table and utilities, you should.

However the majority of those who eventually file for bankruptcy have been struggling along for years trying to pay their debts, scrimping each month to send the minimum, often times either going without basic necessities to do so or else jeopardizing all they hold dear.

What exactly is a bankruptcy and why does the very word strike fear in our heart? Bankruptcy is federally sanctioned debt relief protection under your country's Bankruptcy Code. Doesn't sound so threatening when you put it that way. Actually I really like the "protection" part. It feels rather good after being beat up, and down, for so long. As far as the fear, people fear what they don't understand. There are far more of those who don't understand bankruptcy than those that do. It is this not knowing that is so scary. I will tell you, from my perspective, exactly what a bankruptcy is and how you can not only survive, you can prosper.

Only one who has gone through a situation can truly understand how it feels. Take hope that you too can not only survive a bankruptcy but actually come out better off than if you had never taken that journey in the first place. Adversity makes us dig down deep and discover what we are really made of. What did you ever learn when things were going good?

There are millions of personal stories. Here are three.

CAROLE'S STORY.

I declared bankruptcy in 2003 and emerged from it better off as I learned many lessons from it. I chose to declare Chapter 13 as it allowed me to keep my car and other items purchased on secured loans. I had a great legal firm to work with and for the most part, my creditors respected my decision. Mine wasn't the typical ignore your creditors until they are camped on your doorstep type of bankruptcy. When I filed and a credit report was pulled, I had no late payments or other derogatory remarks. But by this time the cycle had begun, I was living on plastic and basically making a payment so I could use the credit to buy groceries, pay utilities and other necessities. My lawyer, the bankruptcy judge and the trustee commended me for staying afloat as long as I had.

Sure, there were some creditors who suffered in the process but seeing what they are doing to other folks and how they are ripping them off, somehow I don't feel so sorry for them. I think my creditors received something like 1% of the amount owed to them. Surprisingly enough, some creditors never responded, to affirm the amount owed.

With my established repayment record and showing that I was putting forth the effort to learn from my experience, I showed prospective future creditors that I would not be a risk. I purchased a new home at the end of 2005 and a new car in 2007, only two and four years after my bankruptcy. The interest on both are low, which doesn't scream "bankruptcy scars" to me. I have established credit with two major card issuers (without annual fees) and only charge what I can pay off each month. I keep a running budget and keep close tabs on my spending. The biggest lesson learned was learning to live on a budget and within my means.

When people begin to entertain the thought of bankruptcy, they would do well not to talk about it with their friends and family or anyone other than an attorney who specializes in bankruptcy. Most will offer a complimentary consultation to allow the individual the opportunity to obtain enough information to make an informed decision. My attorney stood by me every step of the way and took on any additional issues and really did work for me. The trustee's office had very professional people, never once did I feel like a second class citizen or someone who should be ashamed of having made the choice to file. I had issues such as two IRS bills that I had been making payments on that were rolled into my plan.

Had I talked to anyone other than my attorney, I probably would have chosen to wind up paying thousands of dollars to a debt consolidator or debt settlement company who wouldn't have helped in the long run. I hope my story helps someone who may be on the fence about filing.

RILEY'S STORY.

I was never talked to a lot when I was younger about debt. I got my first credit card when I was seventeen. I lived in a small town and felt I had to get out ASAP after I had my daughter at a young age. I felt like I was invincible and didn't need any help. I moved to the city but found I could not afford food, diapers, babysitters, etc. But I had all these credit cards so a lot of the necessities were charged. It was tough being a young single mom. Things started looking up and I got a good job after school and bought my own house when I was only twenty three and still single. I can still make all the payments but after looking at it now almost ten years later and over $40K total in debt (not counting the house), I felt as if I would never get out of debt. I could only make minimum payments and with my daughter now 14, I don't have too much longer before I have to worry about college tuition. So even though I can still make minimum payments, I should do the bankruptcy on my time and do it now versus later when I am not able to make payments at all. I don't want to make my daughter's life miserable because I can't afford things she needs now. I make over $52 K a year and where I live that is good. I should be able to pay cash for whatever I need after filing. I cannot wait to be able to breathe and never use a credit card again.

I am grateful to be learning my lesson while still young, (I am thirty two), so that I can get this over with and live the rest of my life without the stress. I cannot wait!

Oh yeah, I am also glad, although this sounds kind of twisted, that I can share this experience with my daughter so that she can learn from it. Growing up, money was never talked about. We just thought it was all good. I talk to my daughter about all that is going on so that she can understand what happened to me and what not to do. Hopefully, by doing the bankruptcy now I will be able to actually save some money so that I can help her out if she needs it to prevent her from getting into this situation I found myself in. It makes her appreciate things more and not be all about expensive clothes. She dresses nice and is cute as a button in her clearance Old Navy and Kohl's 50% off. LOL. So she has learned how to be a bargain shopper to save money and she has no problem with it like some teenagers might.

KEN AND SHIRLEY'S STORY.

I wanted to share our story and show how easy (or complicated it was depending on how you view it) to get in trouble. We are both retired and have a pretty good income. We both went back to work after retirement just for something to do. We liked working. We improved our late model mobile home with a new kitchen, doing most of the work ourselves. It made the mobile home more desirable but not more saleable. It had been a life long dream to travel around in our mobile home. We could afford it and the gas that went with it. We jumped out and bought a big used unit about a year ago and started prepping it for the way we wanted it and also readying the mobile home and our land to sell.

In the meantime I lost my job in retirement due to a previous injury coming back to haunt me and could no longer stand long hours on my feet or walk the distances required and had to return to retirement. No problem as my wife still had her job but now that's a requirement as we now have the motor home payment too. We put the home and land up for sale. No problem, we only owe less that 50% of what the homes and land in our area have been selling for. Many buyers came and went. They loved the home and the kitchen that we had nearly $22 K into and they loved the location. But nobody came back.

One day I called the bank to find out what was going on. We found out that when we moved our mobile out of a mobile home park where we were renting to our own property, we had voided any VA or FHA loan guarantees and loans that went with it. That was a shock as that did away with a first time buyer and a low down payment requirement.

We also found out that there were few lenders that were even doing loans on mobile homes and land. Many I talked to told me that if the buyer had great credit and could pay 20-30% down against a current appraisal and pay a rate of 8-12% interest, it could be done. Ouch, that hurt.

OK, we are still doing well enough. We can afford everything as long as the wife is still working. We will just wait until times improve and sell later. In the meantime we have a nice motor home to vacation in.

Then my wife developed a medical problem and she could no longer do her job. She quit but they would have terminated her anyway within a short time as she could no longer meet the requirements of the job.

We put the home up for sale at just above what we owed on the land and home itself. We were certain that someone would want it for half of what the two were worth just a few months before, but found no takers when they learned about the down payment required and the high interest rates.

Now we were stuck. Our savings were going down fast, neither of us can work any longer and selling the motor home is not an option either with gas so high. So we called two people that really wanted the home and land and told them if they could just give us a little equity they could assume both. Wrong! Our mobile home lien holder would not allow either one to assume.

However we did manage to sell just the land and at least cleared that note. The buyer had hoped he could buy or assume the mobile but that has not happened yet and it appears the home will need to be removed from the property.

We moved into a rental, turned the motor home into the lien holder and figured that bankruptcy was our only way out. We should not, of course, have bought the motor home without first having sold the home, but hindsight does not work well. Our excellent credit is gone and we are heading into a Chapter 7 filing.

So goes the best laid plans for retirement. At least we have our retirement incomes and we will live OK once this additional debt is gone. We are now both disabled and our plans to travel are now very limited.

I thought that sharing this might make some of you feel a little better about how you got to where you are at right now.

CHAPTER TWO

A HISTORY OF BANKRUPTCY

A sign of the times is the tsunami of bankruptcies that have hit the planet. The global economy is in the dumper and is taking many people with it. Bankruptcy does not play favorites, there are no persons or entities that are immune, from individuals like you and me, to the huge conglomerates. But it does not stop even there. Counties, municipalities and even countries face bankruptcy. No matter that you are just John or Jane Q. Public or Bear Stearns, no one can be smug enough to say "that could never happen to me". If you are reading, we both know different.

This is not a new phenomenon, it is not a product of modern society. It has been around far longer than credit cards have, although the advent of easy credit has made bankruptcies far more common than they were before the credit card explosion in the late 80's and 90's. It seemed as long as you had a pulse, you could get a credit card. You can find references to bankruptcy in the Bible. In the Book of Deuteronomy, 15:11, Moses brings home God's law from the mountain to the Israelites and directs them to forgive debts every seven years. This forgiveness is called the Jubliee.

We can trace bankruptcy back to the Roman Empire. You and I would not have liked to have endured a bankruptcy back then. It was by no means meant to be a fresh start for the debtor. Rather it was entirely punitive, you were going to pay severely for your crime of indebtedness. Debtors were often imprisoned. The word bankruptcy was a Latin word that means "broken bench" or bancus, which was the tradesman's counter, and ruptus, which was the creditors breaking of the counter. It would be a public display of the debtor's shame, done with the intent of shaming and humiliating the debtor. Talk about adding insult to injury.

The Statue of Merchants in 1285 called for the imprisonment of debtors and this was common up until the mid-nineteenth century. Draconian measures were the order of the day for those who could not pay their debts. These included forfeiture of all property, loss of consortium of a spouse, imprisonment and even death.

In 1542, during the reign of Henry VIII, the first bankruptcy law was passed in England. Debtors were viewed as quasi-criminals. In 1570, under Eliabeth I, Henry's daughter, a more comprehensive bankruptcy law was passed. This law laid the basic parameters of the English bankruptcy system and lasted well into the time of the American Revolution.

A debtor could not institute a bankruptcy proceeding, only creditors could. This restriction lasted for three centuries and pointedly sided with the creditor and their aid, not the debtor. Discharge of debts for the debtor was not an option. Bankruptcy was based on the idea of misconduct on the part of the debtor, not on his financial inability to pay, financial troubles were not considered, nor concern for the debtor was extended. They did wrong and they must pay. Guess the powers that be never read the Bible passage about Moses delivering the message from the mount about forgiveness of debts. As there was no discharge of debts, creditors were able, even after bankruptcy, to continue to dunn debtors for the debt. There seemed to be no remedy for the debtor, no clean slate or second chance. Again, so glad I did not live then.

The bankruptcy laws only applied to merchants or business persons, not the ordinary individual. Those people were really at the bottom of the barrel, deemed to be insolvent. The reason bankruptcy was only available to business people is that society viewed bankruptcy as a natural by-product of commerce. Where commerce is involved, there must be credit extended. It would seem even back then that business seemed somehow to escape the stigma of bankruptcy, much like today. "Oh, it is the cost of doing business," they might say. But what about the common man and woman? Never mind that without them there would be no commerce.

Blackstone, the famous barrister, explained:

> "The Law holds it to be an unjustifiable practice, for any person but a trader to encumber himself with debts of any considerable value. If a gentleman, or one in a liberal profession, at the time of contracting his debts, has a sufficient fund to pay then the delay of payment is a species of dishonesty, and a temporary injustice to his creditor; and if, at such time, he has no sufficient fund, the dishonesty and injustice is the greater".

For the next 200 years, Parliament would periodically amend the laws. They became more punitive. The law was given the power to enter your home and seize your property. A favorite punishment was the pillory. Lopping off of an ear was not unheard of either.

The Statue of Anne was passed in 1705, allowing for the discharge of debts for the debtor as long as they cooperated in the proceeding and the creditor agreed to the discharge. This was the first time that any humanitarianism was shown towards a debtor, as long as they were deemed to be honest and through some sort of unfortunate circumstances, they found themselves in debt and unable to pay. However at the same time the law showed some mercy to the unfortunate debtor, it was ratcheting up the stakes to uncooperative debtors by allowing them to be put to death. Not only were they put to death but they were executed without benefit of clergy like any other felon. Bankruptcy was viewed as a property crime and property crime was considered heinous enough to warrant the death penalty. The death penalty could be, and was, applied to debtors during the 115 years that it was on the books. History documents that in reality no more than five debtors were actually put to death, not so bad, unless of course you happened to be one of the five.

Around the middle 1700's, a more liberal view was taken towards debtors, although the laws remained very pro-creditor, not pro-debtor. The American Revolution was largely responsible for this shift in attitude.

Blackstone writes in 1765:

> "A bankrupt.....formerly considered merely in the light of a criminal... but at present the laws of bankruptcy are considered as laws calculated for the benefit of trade, and founded on the principles of humanity as well as justice: and to that end they confer some privileges, not only on the creditors, but also on the debtor or bankrupt himself".

The United States bankruptcy laws are based upon British bankruptcy statutes from the sixteenth century. Bankruptcy was meant to be a punishment, not the second chance it is today. The original thirteen colonies, being British subjects, based their bankruptcy laws upon the British system. Bankruptcy got a little less punitive during this time, debtors could actually be allowed to retain some of their possessions, although imprisonment was still very much a threat.

The United States Constitution tried to make the bankruptcy law more uniform throughout the country and favor started to swing to the debtor and away from the creditor. With a creditor's approval, a debtor could have his debt discharged. These laws favoring debtors fueled a huge outcry and subsequently several of the acts favoring debtors were repealed. But no matter, the seeds were sown that led to today's bankruptcy framework. Both you and I should be grateful that we are living in this time in history where we can go on to live a much better life, as opposed to being imprisoned or killed.

The first federal bankruptcy law was passed on April 4, 1800, eleven years after the constitution was ratified. The crash of 1792 had caused an outcry for a national bankruptcy law but it was not until the panic of 1797 occurred, bringing widespread ruin and prisons bursting at the seams with debtors, that a federal law was finally passed. One notable prisoner was Robert Morris, who helped finance the American Revolution to the tune of twelve million dollars. He paid with three years of his life in a debtor's prison. This law passed by a single vote. A discharge was finally available to a debtor, as long as they cooperated. An agreement by two thirds of the creditors was also necessary. But before long, an outcry was raised for the repeal of this act. One of the reasons was that many of the benefactors of this law were high flying speculators who used the bankruptcy relief by betting the bank and if it failed, just declaring bankruptcy and starting over again. Not much has changed. Bankruptcy was being used as a business model even way back then. It was also around this time imprisonment for debt was being phased out. But they were still not entitled to a discharge. Debtors did not have to worry about going to prison but they were still unable to escape persecution by creditors. And we know what persecution from creditors is like. So no imprisonment but no peace either.

Enter the Bankruptcy Act of 1841. Now we are getting somewhere. This was a most important act in the history of bankruptcy. It allowed for the first time that the debtor was allowed to file for bankruptcy, previously a privilege reserved for the creditor. Not only that, the debtor could finally receive a discharge. However the many conditions attached made it difficult for the debtor to comply but at least there was the glimmer of hope for freedom from creditor persecution. Alas, this law was repealed in 1843, only two short years, but not before a multitude of debtors were saved.

What one might call the first modern bankruptcy act was finally passed, the Bankruptcy Act of 1898. This was the law of the land for eighty years and was unique in many ways. It recognized the credit economy that was emerging due to the Industrial Age. Now here was an act that concentrated on the debtor rather than the creditor. It allowed the debtor a complete discharge of debts and many more exemptions of assets than ever before. While this act focused on liquidation of assets, it also introduced a new concept, a reorganization process for saving distressed businesses. This act was a watershed moment in history for debtors. It favored debtors with liberal treatment, liberal being a relative term. The tide was turning. While earlier acts had allowed for a discharge, there were so many conditions to be met and grounds for denial, it was pretty ineffective for the debtor. This act abolished the restrictions and limited the grounds mandatory for the discharge, all welcome news.

The Chandler Act of 1938 introduced Chapters Ten and Eleven. This was extraordinary progress. It enabled businesses to reorganize instead of liquidating. This reorganization in lieu of liquidation idea would find its way to the many debtors, like myself, in the form of the eventual Chapter 13 bankruptcy.

During the Great Depression in the United States, the credit industry tried to call foul. They were not happy with the discharge allowing debtors to get off without trying to pay any of their debts off or at least a percentage. The Depression was not a good time to try and get Congress to change what the credit industry considered to be liberal handling of debtors in favor of making the debtors make some kind of repayment. How do you browbeat debtors to repay their debts when the country is in the midst of a great depression, when it was all people could do to keep a roof over their heads and food on their tables. The credit industry was fighting a losing battle.

The Bankruptcy Reform Act of 1978 issued in modern bankruptcy. It was the first bankruptcy legislation that had not been enacted as the result of an economic depression and the first major reform since the Bankruptcy Act of 1898. This act was major for debtors, a real victory. It introduced legislation allowing for the consumer to reorganize under the Code without having to lose everything and in some cases without losing anything. This was called a Chapter 13.

This act sought to encourage and support the Chapter 13 bankruptcy for the individual as Chapter 10 and 11 did for business. Chapter 13 was a repayment plan of sorts. The premise is that this would be a real fresh start. Creditors would be able to recoup a portion of their losses and the debtor would walk away with what they owned and better credit.

For the first time in history bankruptcy was accepted and sanctioned by law to be a clean slate, a second chance in life.

The next and last reform of the bankruptcy laws came in 2005, pushed through in large part to the credit card companies and their powerful lobbyists. They thought that far too many consumers were abusing the bankruptcy laws. It had become almost too easy to rack up a lot of debt and walk away unscathed, except for a damaged credit report for a measly few years.

To try and stem this tide of abuse, the Bankruptcy Act of 2005 was meant to impose stricter guidelines for those seeking protection. It sought to identify the differences between Chapter 7, 11, and 13 Bankruptcy.

Chapter 7 deals with unsecured debts, credit cards, medical bills and unsecured loans This is often referred to as the liquidation bankruptcy. You are required to liquidate your assets but only assets you have equity in and even then some part of your equity is sheltered. So in effect you could possibly file Chapter 7, wipe out all your credit cards and still keep all your property and assets.

Chapter 11 is for business seeking bankruptcy protection. Chrysler is a good example. Chrysler can file a Chapter 11, reorganize, restructure the debt and continue on, almost like nothing had ever happened. Many companies are operating today with just that scenario.

Chapter 13 is a plan to restructure an individual's debt, much like Chapter 11 does for business. This plan is a repayment plan. However it is not based on what you owe the creditor, rather it is based on what you can legitimately afford to pay and not end up living in your car. A debtor is allowed, providing you have a steady income, to keep property that you otherwise would have lost. If you do not have a steady income, for instance if you have a commission based job, do yourself a favor. Get a job with a regular paycheck. It is a small price to pay for what you will reap. The court approves a repayment plan that allows you to pay a portion of your debt off in a three to five year plan of making a set payment each month.

Your repayment plan in a Chapter 13 is arrived at by taking your income minus your expenses. Whatever you have left over is the amount you make to the plan. I can almost hear you thinking, "what leftover money?" But it works, it worked for me and it will for you. More on that in a later chapter. After the period of three to five years, (almost sounds like a prison sentence but it is anything but) as long as you have made agreed upon payments, your bankruptcy will be discharged. You may think three to five years is a long time but the alternative is real ugly and if you are like me, you will bless the check you send each month to the trustee. Not only is this your one way ticket out of debt row hell, you are getting your future back.

Income qualifiers are needed. If you have the money to pay back any part of your debt, no matter how small the percentage, you do not have the option of a Chapter 7, instead you must file a Chapter 13.

All filers are required to take credit card counseling. Painless, quick and cheap. You can take the counseling online at a cost of about $70. Then you have to talk to a counselor by phone for some very basic counseling on money management. The counselor sends you your certificate and you can check that off your list.

You are also allowed to keep IRA's, pension accounts, employee annuities and stock bonus plans. So for all you out there who are depleting these very precious commodities to pay off credit card debt, you might want to rethink that.

Some educational loans can be wiped out, provided you can prove that by paying this loan back it would cause you a financial hardship. A Chapter 13 bankruptcy also mandates that you must file a financial restructuring plan within 120 days of filing and it must be accepted by the court within 180 days. This is nothing more than a budget. Income in, income out. You must list monies coming in each month and what you pay each month for the mortgage, food, utilities, car payments, clothes and any other monies going out. The court obviously does not expect the debtor to live a stark, strip downed life. On the worksheet they give you to fill out, cable and entertainment were included in the line items. The financial restructuring plan is pretty much the end product of your petition application so give great thought to filling out the paperwork for your petition.

I did not include this history lesson to bore you but rather to frame this whole concept in a historical perspective. I found that studying bankruptcy in the context of history was very comforting. Take heart that there indeed is "nothing new under the sun". You are not unusual or unique, except hopefully in your own mind. You may feel like you are alone and the only person who could possibly know how awful this feels but people have been in the same situation for centuries. Just thank the powers that be that we are living in this time in history. When you are going through this painful realization that you are in way over your heard and are swiftly on your way to going under, it helps to know that this is not a new phenomenon. We have had a lot of company down through the ages who have faced one of life's most significant crisis.

This thought comforts me as I hope it does you. As they survived and prospered, so can we. We can find ourselves in a place we could never have imagined during the darkest days, struggling under the crushing burden of debts with no hope of escape.

CHAPTER THREE

A FUNNY THING HAPPENED ON THE WAY TO BANKRUPTCY

Like so many people today we got into a severe debt situation. It seems like we all have to run so much faster just to stay in the same place and no matter how fast we run, sometimes we get run over, and that is just for pure survival. Add our lust for consumerism to that mix and we are in big trouble. Even if we were not ravenous consumers, who left to our own devices would find ourselves circling the newest game boy like sharks who had been on a plankton diet, we cannot escape the constant bombardment of commercial consumerism, hawking at us from every conceivable source.

One only has to park themself in front of the television, remote in hand, and flip through the stations. You will surely find commercials hawking everything from personal hygiene products to help you catch a mate, to Hummers, to make you feel like a big man or woman who just snagged that parking space two steps from the mall so as to not have to walk too far and get to shopping faster and probably using plastic to pay for it. There are just too many sources out there ready to fight tooth and nail to part you from your money. Even without the constant inducements, whether blatant or subliminal, we being of human nature always want more. We as consumers will never have all our needs and wants met, even if we could actually be honest and separate out our needs from our wants. The powers that be seduce us ever so delicately, (or not) into over-consuming, over-indulging and just plain over the moon when it comes to spending money.

So far I have only been talking about discretionary spending. How about the debt we find ourselves in due to job loss, divorce, medical emergencies or a myriad of other reasons that have nothing to do with the latest electronic gadget that we, or our child, must have. A woman who desperately wanted a child spent $75,000 on fertility treatments, charged to her credit cards.

The treatments failed to produce a pregnancy. Now she has a $75,000 debt and still no baby. How about when we have to charge the groceries or we don't eat this week? How many times have we used credit because we did not have money to get what we needed just to survive. How is that for irony, we need to charge because we have no money. But when the bill comes in with interest, late fees, hidden fees and whatever else the credit card industry can sock you for, well then you really can't afford it and here you are in another month needing the same things you did last month, starting the insidious cycle all over again. No wonder so many of us find ourselves in a huge hole with little hope of ever climbing out.

This is where I found myself, in that hole, with no chance of escape. There is a scene in the movie "*The Perfect Storm*". The character Mark Wallberg plays finds himself tossed into a raging sea after his ship has sunk. He is this tiny little dot being tossed around by the giant waves. He knows he has no chance and will die and there is nothing in the world that will save him. That is how I felt, just like that little dot, flung about by the waves. It matters not how you got where you are with consumer debt. The result is the same whether you got there because of over-consumption or because of one of life's adversities visiting itself upon you. Our debt problem was caused by a business venture that my husband and I undertook. In hindsight it was evident we were in way over our heads.

For years we had had an on going love affair with real estate. We had very ambitious plans. My husband had the maintenance/building skills and I had the business and financial skills, it was a good partnership. Our idea of fun was making money by buying and fixing properties. We would buy up houses on the cheap, foreclosures, estates and just plain junkers in desperate need of rehab. Finding properties that would increase our bottom line was not work to us, it was an adventure and something we could do together as a couple. We did very well at it too. During this time we both had 9-5 jobs, just regular middle class, middle of the road people, but people with a burning desire to get out of the 9-5 rat race and make it on our own with our real estate investing business.

We bought our first investment property, an estate sale, around Christmas. Someone asked me what I got for Christmas and I told them "I got a house". Sure beats jewelry. I got a money making vehicle. We refinanced our home to take out money for the down payment. At the closing I remember signing my name on the closing documents and thinking I hoped we knew what we were doing.

Many people have done well in real estate investing but it could also turn out badly. Borrowing against the family home to finance the venture, no less. But hey, nothing ventured, nothing gained. So we plunged right in.

We spent many hours and days cleaning, painting, and turning the neglected house into a warm and inviting place where anyone would be happy to live. The plan was to fix it up, raise the value and sell it. We were looking at a profit of about $20,000 after capital gains tax and closing costs. Not bad when you consider we were making a combined salary of about $50,000 a year. Just about the time we finished and were getting ready to sell it, I did some math. I figured that if we held the house for ten years, rented it, enjoyed the appreciation and the tax breaks, we would make much more than $20,000. So we decided to rent it for $650 a month. The total mortgage, including taxes and insurance, was $385, leaving us a cash flow every month of $265. After a year that would be $3180 and after ten years that would be $31,800. And that was just cash flow, there would still be the appreciation, the amortization and the tax breaks. We kept the property and refinanced it to gain capital to buy two more properties and do the same thing. We just kept duplicating that formula and amassing more properties.

Eventually we had enough properties that we had an extra $2500 a month coming in as cash flow. I quit my 9-5 job and got a real estate license and concentrated on finding more properties for our real estate investment business. Quitting my job was something that I had yearned for, freedom and autonomy, no more punching a time clock, trading my precious hours for a measly paycheck. We were making money and having a great time.

We decided it was time to build our dream house in the country. Based on our net worth due to all our investments, the bank happily handed over the money to build. We were the general contractors and were planning on doing a lot of the work ourselves. It took us a good two years to get it done but we were able to live in it while we were doing the work. Living in a house while it's under construction was challenging. When we moved in on a cold winters' day, it had no back door, just a piece of vinyl covering the opening. Being that we were in the country, I did worry about critters coming in. There was no plumbing or toilet, but there was a port a potty sixty feet away from the house. The kitchen was a camp stove, a refrigerator, a utility tub, a microwave and a George Forman. Take out helped us get by too.

The floors would go down last so for the longest time the floors were bare, just the plain old particle board that is used in building. Whenever it got dirty I would just paint it. A carpet layer friend gave us several large remnants to at least cover the floor so we were not walking on bare wood. But no matter, it was well worth it, and strange as it seems, it was fun, it was an adventure. I did not lament my having to "put up with" the situation, as inconvenient as it was. I thought that I would rather have accomplished what we did, on our own, than have had someone hand me the keys to a brand new house all done and ready. What would have been the satisfaction in that? But the majority of people could have not, or not wanted to, go through all that effort and work. They would have opted for someone handing them the keys.

We then decided that since we just built a house and obviously knew what we were doing, we would, instead of buying older houses to rehab, build instead a new apartment building. We did some market research and determined that handicapped housing for the older tenant would be a good investment. With the baby boomer generation approaching that demographic, the market was ripe for that type of housing.

We got to work getting the construction proposal together for the bank. It was an exhaustive and complex procedure. We had found the perfect piece of property, located next to a metro park and near a hospital, shopping, a golf course and the lake. Now all we had to do was get all the bids from the subcontractors and make a construction budget to present to the bank from which they would make a determination of the loan amount needed. It was a painstaking and tricky task. If the bids were too high, the construction costs might be too high, cutting into profits. In real estate investing, the money is made on the buy, the front end. If the bids were too low, the budget would be short, causing trouble of another kind.

For the months it took us to work on the proposal, every waking moment was consumed with the task. We had a lot riding on this investment and we were a little nervous by the enormity of the step we were taking. It was all we thought about, talked about and spent our time on.

We just about had the proposal finished and were getting ready to submit it to the bank. We were waiting on one bid, that from the electrician. He promised to come over the day before the proposal was due to give me his bid. He said he would be over at noon and when he hadn't shown up by 6:00 I was frantic.

I kept calling him on his cell phone with no luck. Finally about 9:00 that night he called. So sorry, he said, but he had been in a fatal car accident and had been at the hospital all day. "You are still coming over right?" I blurted out. As soon as the words were out I realized how obsessed I had become. That must have sounded terrible. The stress had turned me into someone I did not even know. If I only knew that was a harbinger of things to come.

As we already had a good track record at the bank, we had no trouble securing the loan. We had never tackled such a big project but were confident based on what we had been able to accomplish so far. So we jumped right in. We were going to do much of the work ourselves to save money. As I had never been accused of lacking an ego, I was confident we could pull it off and become financially independent for life. Such hubris would come back to haunt me.

Even though we had borrowed the money for the construction, I knew that unexpected expenses always come up. As we did not have much of a reserve of cash, I opened up as many lines of credit as I could, just in case. Since our credit was so very good, I had no trouble. I got huge lines of credit all with very good interest rates. Did I worry about paying for this money? No, not at all. The building had been appraised significantly higher than the loan, so we had a good equity position. When the building was done we would just refinance and take care of any additional costs we might incur. Even with additional expenses, this would be a money making proposition.

We had no sooner gotten started when our first unexpected expense not covered in the budget showed up. When I got the bid for the sewer it said the cost would be $825 so that was the amount for that line item. When I went to the sewer department to pay the $825, I got a nasty surprise. The fee was $825 for EACH unit. The total cost was actually $9900. I had missed that and so had the bank. OK this was not the time to panic, thank goodness I had thought to take out those lines of credit, fifteen to be exact. Crisis averted, we had to keep the project moving ahead. This would be the first in a long line of emergencies that were financed by the "credit card shuffle".

The subcontractor we had hired to clear the land and prepare it for building kept putting us off. A big part of the problem was that he knew we were inexperienced in commercial construction and we would just take it instead of scrambling to find another contractor who would do it at the price he had quoted. He was right. Finally the day came when we went to the site and he was at long last clearing the land. But wait, you knew it couldn't be that easy. As every square inch of the land was covered with trees, brush, rocks and debris, the actual land was not visible. After clearing everything off the land, a sandstone foundation was discovered. Do you know how much it costs to excavate sandstone and haul it away? Well neither did we but we found out. Another huge expense that was not covered in the budget. But not to panic, remember the plan, that's what the lines of credit are for. When the building was done we would refinance and pay off the additional costs. For now we would do what we had to do to keep the building moving ahead. We could not make any money until it was done and rented.

By the time the land was cleared and ready for the foundation to be laid, it was winter. Can't pour concrete in the winter, or so the concrete contractor said. Too risky, he explained. So several more months went down the drain while waiting for the foundation to be poured. We were at a standstill and being a type A personality, it was killing me. But in the meantime the bank was, of course, expecting its' payment. With a construction loan you only pay interest on the amount of the loan that you have drawn on so far. At the end of six months the loan was due to roll over into the permanent loan with the full mortgage and the foundation hadn't even been laid yet. How were we going to pay a full loan payment? We had no rents coming because we had no building to rent, just a big plot of earth.

I asked the bank for a six month extension, explaining in great detail all the delays, and they agreed. That gave us a little breathing room and hey, spring is not far behind, we will just have to make up for lost time.

After almost a full year to the day, the foundation was poured. It was a beautiful sight. This was the first tangible evidence that eventually a building would stand on this plot of earth.

Finally we are on our way. For a while things seemed to be actually moving forward, instead of backwards or standing still. The carpenters started framing and I actually dared to hope we could pull this off. For some time I had been questioning the wisdom of taking on such a project. I asked myself "what was I thinking?" This was more and more looking like a situation where we had bit off more than we can chew. But we were in it now and there was no turning back.

There is something heart warming about seeing walls and roofs going up and on. No more delays or surprises. Yeah sure. At right about this honeymoon phase, another nasty surprise showed itself. Contrary to what we had been led to believe by the seller of the property, there was no gas or water on the property. Again our fault, we failed to do our due diligence. The gas company came out and told us it would cost $10,000 to lay the gas lines to service all the units. Then the water company came out and informed us that to get water to the property it would cost $7800. Oh, yeah and you also need a pit for the meter. How much is a pit? About $1100.

This would have been almost funny if not so serious. As we did not put these costs in the construction budget, we were left to come up with this money. Another big hit to the credit cards. But that is why we got them. We didn't like it much but what else could we do. We believed we would still come out ahead, even with these additional expenses. We were convinced that this building would be a goldmine and set us up for life, so quit whining already and get that money off the credit cards. Hey if this was easy, anybody could do it. But we weren't just anybody, we were "us" and we were going to make this work if it killed us.

Through the summer the carpenters worked and at last it finally started looking like an apartment building. They got it framed, roofed and sided, windows and exterior doors hung and the interior walls were up by fall. We still did not have any heat or water and we needed water to mix the drywall mud. We just improvised and got a large industrial water tank. We had to truck in the water for the tank so the drywall contractor could finish the walls.

We had gotten two bids for the drywall work. One was for $47,000 and one for $26,000. We took the lower bid. But by the time we were ready for the drywall, that contractor had retired. Since we only had $26,000 in the budget for drywall, I needed to find someone who would do the job for that amount. I went back to the contractor who had given us the $47,000 bid and asked him to come over to talk about doing the job for us. I was going to ply him with Corona and promise him all future drywall work if he would do the job for $26,000. Hey, it worked. I must admit however, after he left, I felt just a tad sleazy but I needed to plug that $21,000 hole. It reminded me of the scene in "*The Money Pit*" where the character Tom Hanks plays tells his girlfriend, played by Shelly Long, maybe she should be nice to the contractor, especially since he has a brother that is a plumber.

Now we are really getting somewhere. But wait, another winter would soon be upon us. We were desperate to get the building done by winter because that is never a good time to move, especially for my target market, the older tenant. If only I could get one unit done and use it as a model, I could at least get some deposits to help with our cash flow problem.

Our debt was mushrooming. I was being very creative though. I would pay one credit card with another by transferring a balance. Because we had fifteen credits you can imagine all the activity going back and forth on all these cards. It was almost a full time job just keeping up with shuffling finances. But hey, I wasn't too worried, remember I had a plan. It would all work out, just as soon as we get this darned building done, get the units rented and start receiving rents. I just prayed that the house of cards, the credit card house of cards, held out.

Last, but certainly not least, our full mortgage note was about to come due. The monthly amount was several thousand dollars. Now that was going to be a problem. I felt like we were trapped in some nether world with no hope of ever seeing the light of day.

At last, one unit was ready to show as a model. We still had no heat so we were using space heaters for heat. Of course since we did not have electricity either, I had to run a very long extension cord out the window and up to the temporary electric pole out back and hope they don't notice. The parking lot was a huge mud hole as the paving of the lot would be the last thing done. It was about that time that I realized that we had failed to include a line item in the budget for a parking lot. Again, one I had missed and apparently so had the bank. But can't worry about that one right now, there are enough other pressing issues to deal with. I will cross that bridge when I come to it, then maybe throw myself over.

By this time all logic had flown out the window, stress can do that. No matter that the units were not ready to rent, don't you know how badly I needed them to be ready, as if just needing it could will it to be so. I was possessed. All these months of robbing Peter to pay Paul, with no end in sight, and now I was running out of Peter.

I opened the model for the world to see, hoping they would not pay too much attention to the shortfalls mentioned above. I knew when they saw how beautiful the model looked, after spending $500 on staging courtesy of

Discover, they would whip out their checkbooks and put a deposit down on a unit that I would assure them would be ready "any day now".

It always amazes me the lack of vision most people have. Not one person wanted to rent an apartment. Couldn't they imagine how it would be to live there once the heavy duty extension cord was removed when the electric service was installed. I guess not.

Well that was a major blow and another winter was almost here, not the best time for construction in the northeast. Another winter faced with an unfinished and unoccupied building with the meter running. More months of mortgage payments to come, fed by more months of credit card debt. But hey, we're still here, plugging along with never a thought of giving up. It reminded me of the scene in the movie *"Pappion"* when the character played by Steve McQueen is thrown into a pit of solitary confinement as punishment for trying to escape. Day after day a guard would walk by the pit and peer in and Steve McQueen would defiantly growl at him "I'm still here, you bastards".

The original plan was to subcontract out a lot of the work. My husband was still working his full time job and every waking minute he was not at work, he would be working at the apartments. It became clear we did not have the financial luxury of hiring the work needed to finish the interior. This meant we would have to do the painting, hang doors and cabinets, finish plumbing and electric and lay floors. Of course by we I really meant him. I didn't sign up for this. But I would be right there behind him all the way. The good news was that by doing the work ourselves, we could pay ourselves from the construction budget.

Things were looking up. Of course this meant for a grueling schedule, especially for my husband. I could help out by cleaning and painting but the bulk of this work fell to him. He would work from 8 to 5 at his job and then go to the apartments and work until late at night, come home exhausted and cold, fall into bed, get up and start all over. As we still only had temporary electric, he had huge, and heavy, 100 foot extension cords strung through the units for electricity. But still no heat. And this was in the winter. He did set up a torpedo heater to keep the unit warm while working in it.

We still had no water so he would have to haul it from home. Talk about roughing it. This was one of the longest winters of our lives, but hey, spring can't be too far behind. Got to have optimism.

After going around and around in my head about the budget, I realized there would be no way we could finish this project with the construction budget that we had, we needed more money. But from where and from whom could we possibly get it? Now I was getting panicky. I mentally ticked off my options and they were none too enticing. I could try and borrow it from family. Discounted that almost immediately, never mix family and business. Maybe I could find a hard money lender, I call them Guido, not really a route I wanted to take. We had come too far to fail but a solution was proving to be elusive. We had come so far but still not far enough. We had run out of money and we were running out of credit. If we couldn't finish, we couldn't refinance and without the money from the refinance, we would not be able to pay off the credit card debt.

Then it hit me. Who, besides us, has an investment in this project? Why didn't I think of that before, the bank of course. I screwed up my courage and called the head of the mortgage loan department, I was going straight to the top. I told him about our situation and asked him to come out the next day to see what we had accomplished and what we still needed to bring this project, finally, to fruition.

The next day was a bone chilling, windy and raw day. I invited him to come into the model to show off what we had accomplished to date. We still had no heat so it was almost as cold inside as it was outside. But it looked good, even if you could see your breath as you talked. And I talked. I told him that we needed more money to finish the project and hoped the bank would see it that way too. He was pretty non-committal, just walked around peering here and there. As he turned towards the door to walk out he said over his shoulder, "put a budget together of what was still needed and submit it to the bank". That was close enough to a yes for me, I knew they would approve it. As he stood with his hand on the doorknob, anxious to get back to his warm car, he stopped and looked at me and told me something shocking. He said I was a terrific salesperson, so good in fact that when our loan had originally come before the board, there were some who voted against giving us the loan, citing our inexperience in commercial construction. He told me I had sold the project so well they overlooked our inexperience and made the loan. That was the first time I had heard that our loan has just squeaked by. Wow, look at how close we had come to missing all this!

I got all the bids and budget together post haste and presented it to the bank, where they would vote on it. As we sat in front of the loan officer going over our application, I felt like a kid in the principal's office. She would look at the paperwork, look at the computer then look at us. I was on pins and needles, fearing she was going to find something in those papers or on the computer. She said the application would be submitted to the board and we would know in about a week.

A few days later the bank called to say they had approved the additional money, $40,000. I was just going to ask for $30,000 but they encouraged me to get the number up, better that there was a cushion. They added they did not want me coming back a third time. That made two of us. Well all right, if you insist. At least we would have a cushion if more unexpected expenses came up. If?

When we went in to sign the final papers they explained that the new loan was an equity line of credit and that they never do that for construction loans but they were making an exception in our case. Maybe I am a better salesperson than I thought. They said that the interest would be 9% and they stressed the 9% lest I not understand. I'm thinking, I would not care at this point if it were 20%. All I knew is we needed the money now to finish the project so that we can refinance and pay off the credit card debt accrued thanks to a six month project taking two years.

I was feeling pretty good at this point, what the heck. Through all the challenges that we had been through we never gave up, and we never would. Many people would have thrown up their hands and walked away from the project from hell. But not us.

After what seemed like another endless winter and feeling like we were in this deep dark and cold place, finally it was spring. We got our first tenant. When that deposit check came in the mail, I held it in my hand and cried.

Our first tenant was due to move in. Renting that first unit was a milestone. I remember the day well. I was at the apartment bright and early to welcome the tenant and give her the keys. I am a firm believer, contrary to what many landlords think, that allowing tenants to have a pet is a good thing. People love their pets and if you refuse to rent to pet owners, you are cutting out a large segment of the potential tenant pool. We not only allow pets, we welcome them. We stress welcome in our marketing, it is not that ok yeah we will allow your pet, but rather we welcome your pet. There's a difference. It works. The worst case scenario is that you keep their deposit. I far greater fear a vacant unit than fear a pet soiling the carpet.

I opened the door and ushered the tenant and her little dog into the apartment that we were so very proud of. The first thing the little dog did was squat on the carpet and do his business. I do believe I gasped. The tenant was very apologetic, I airily waved it off, saying the little guy was just excited. OK at that point I didn't even care, we had a paying tenant.

By this time my husband had actually moved into one of the units. We live about 20 miles from the job site and that made for a long drive home after working thirteen hours. We now had water, gas and electric. It had been two years since we started, two very long and vexing years. A six month project was now two years old. The extra expense we incurred was off the charts. The credit card balances had grown, a lot. While I knew my plan to pay off the debt by the new financing on the building was a good solid plan, good enough that I never worried about repaying this debt, it was still a precipitous position to be in. It was a constant balancing act, the logistics were tricky. I used to feel like I was juggling balls in the air. Then I moved onto balancing plates, much harder. The plates had to be balanced just right, all monies moving along as they should be, all construction details being taken care of.

After we had built our house and decided that hey that wasn't so hard, let's build an apartment building, how much harder can that be? Could we have been that naïve? I will be the first to admit that our inexperience and stupidity were very instrumental in all the problems that dogged us during this project. But you learn by doing. Yes it was costing us far more than we thought and we would be leveraged up to the hilt for years to come, yet I stubbornly held onto the belief that it was still a good idea and it would all work out and make us prosperous in the long run. We just have to hang in there. There was a lot of weight hanging on our shoulders and we knew it.

So what did we do? We went to Mexico. That's right. After working for almost two years, thirteen hours a day, with the only day taken off being Christmas, we decided, darn it all, we need, no we deserve a break. So off we went to Mexico for a week of sun and relaxation on a white sand beach with impossibly colored water and lots of buckets of Coronas with lime. A good friend of mine, good enough that I shared with her our burgeoning debt situation, asked me how we could afford that. I answered her that when you are thousands upon thousands of dollars in debt, what is another two thousand? We needed it, we deserved it and we took it.

It must have been that Mexican vacation but all of the sudden the momentum started to turn our way and things started happening. I spent every day that summer at the apartments working. For a person who pretty much disdains physical work, I was quite proud of myself. As an extra bonus for working so hard, I lost twenty pounds. I had been trying for years, just took a little old fashioned physical labor, ugh, to do it.

One by one we were renting the apartments. Finally, I think the finish line will soon be in sight. Every time I rented a unit, it was one step closer. We planned to be done by September at which time we would get the new financing. So close, but as it turns out, not close enough.

I had been doing a pretty good job of juggling the credit cards and the payments. Almost everything that had been put on credit was either a cash advance to feed the project or building materials above and beyond what was covered in the budget. Oh don't forget the $2000 for the Mexican vacation. Hey that was a work related cost, if the help did not get some relief from the work and stress soon, they might have a breakdown and then where would they be?

With all those credit card bills coming in at all different times of the month I spent a lot of time watching the balances, transferring the balances, making sure minimum payments were paid and paid on time. I had gotten real good at this unique application of the shell game. However I was soon to find out, and am sure it is stated in that minuscule print that you see on your credit card agreement, that they can raise your rates anytime they want to. As long as I paid the minimum payment, there was no problem and I was able to do that. One day I opened a bill from a credit card that was carrying the highest balance, about $20,000. They were raising my interest rate from 11% to 32%, just like that. After I stopped sputtering and choking, I called them and asked them why they had raised my interest rate. They replied that when a customer's balance gets high, whether they have been keeping up or not, they can automatically raise the interest rate. "So that is supposed to help me how?", I asked. No answer. I then asked the customer service representative if the company knew that loan sharking was illegal. They did not care much for that statement. So now my minimum payment of $300 a month, which I had been managing to pay, jumped to $737 a month, which I was not able to pay, not and pay all the other fourteen too. And just like dominos, several of our other credit card companies raised our rate, which raised our payment, which now I could not make. And we had only about a month or two to go before we would be able to get refinanced. The best laid plans and all, you know. So close, yet it still keeps moving out of reach.

It was now a race to the finish, what would happen first, default on the credit card payments or the completion of the building and the new financing. We went ahead and started the application for the refinancing with assurance to the bank that it would be totally finished and fully occupied by September. Then the waiting started. It had to again go before the board. It did not enter my mind that they would not approve it, so far we had gotten everything we had asked for. Yes I knew we missed the July and August payment to the credit card company, the one with the $787 minimum payment at 32%. I was sure I could explain that away so I was not overly concerned.

One night about a week later the phone rang. It was the banker. I thought he was calling to congratulate us on a job well done and thank us for providing such a valuable service to the community and when could they possibly start lending us money again and how much did I think we would need. However the tone of his voice stopped me cold. He was very polite and apologetic but he informed me the bank would not be refinancing our building due to our debt load being, well pretty much off the charts and because our credit rating had taken a huge dive because of the missed credit card payments. I told him he didn't under-stand, the building was to be collateral and with the new financing our credit card debt would be wiped off, the amount being amortized into the new loan. Uh no, apparently they did not see it that way. The banker was so very sorry and he wanted to deliver the bad news to me by phone rather than by mail. I numbly thanked him and hung up. This was the worst possible news I could hear. I just sat there holding the dead phone in my hand, stunned.

My mind started searching frantically for a Plan B, got to have a Plan B. Boy I really did it this time. The hard part was I had to conceal my panic and not let onto my husband the very dangerous financial position we were in. My husband really had no clue as to the true nature of our financial crisis. The finances had always been left in my hands and we both liked it that way. I did not need him worried about the finances, I needed him focused on getting the work done. I could not let him know how bad things really were and telling him would only worry him and what would that accomplish? I have a theory when it comes to tell or don't tell. I ask myself, would telling help the situation or hinder the situation? Clearly sharing with him my panic would not change a thing and it would only makes things worse. I would keep this blow to myself and try to figure out an answer. I have usually been able to "pull things out of the hat" and felt confident that I could find some lender, maybe a little less discriminating, to give us new financing.

Maybe you see yourself in a similar situation. Many spouses hide their true indebtedness from the other. Money is without a doubt the one thing that spouses fight about above all other, before even sex and children. I was lucky, there were no fights about money as he was in the dark. Even if he knew though, he would trust me to take care of the situation. And I was going to do just that.

The good news was that the building was done and fully rented. While this should have been the cause for much rejoicing, I was far too worried to celebrate and could not even enjoy our great accomplishment, against all odds.

CHAPTER FOUR

A FUNNY THING HAPPENED..........
PART TWO

There is a distinct line of demarcation in my story at this point. The past two years had been filled to overflowing with crisis, worry and stress that I probably would have been laughing about if I wasn't busy crying. It was like a comedy of errors, the theatre of the absurd. If something could go wrong, it surely did. Between the unexpected expenses, to weather delays to the contractors raking us over the coals to the constant struggle to find and shuffle money around to make this whole thing work, I was at my wit's end. Of course we had our life's savings riding on this project. No, no pressure there. It often felt like we were bailing out the Titanic with a teaspoon. Now at last we were done. What irony, what should have been cause for celebration turned immediately into a heart stopping panic.

The huge credit debt we were carrying never bothered me too much as there was the PLAN. Yes I would cringe every time a credit card statement arrived proclaiming our balance was $17,000. Seeing your balance in the five figure range tends to shake you up a bit. But I knew once we were done and obtained the new financing on the building we would be in good shape. Even with all the delays and their attendant costs, we would still have an excellent investment. We just would not have as much equity as we had planned on but we would still be better off than if we had not taken this project on. This was never intended to be a get rich quick plan. We would hold this investment property for the rest of our lives, having the tenants pay off the mortgage. This was our retirement plan, the ultimate 401K. With the new financing we would be able to pay off all the credit card debt and be well positioned for a secure future and retirement. All of our hard work and sacrifice would have been well worth it.

Ah, the best laid plans and all that.....

Now I was in cold hard territory. This was a totally alien fear to me. This fear was raw, it was fear that I had never known. It was the fear of financial disaster, the fear of losing everything we had worked so hard for through the years.

I started looking to other lenders, maybe find one more sympathetic to our plight. When they pulled up our credit report, the conversation was pretty much over. They all said that our credit scores has plummeted, due to the missed payments we had incurred when the loan sharks had tripled our payments plus the huge debt load we were carrying. While I tried to explain what happened, they were not interested. Underwriting guidelines prevail. Your FICA score is the Holy Grail and no explanations or excuses are considered. We had gone from being gold to being crap, gone from lenders trying to throw money at us to lenders not returning calls.

This was the first time in my life I had been totally stumped. My ego had lulled me into believing there was nothing I could not do, nothing I could not pull off if needed. The fear gnawed my mind, the agony gnawed my gut. You may know the feeling. This was an impossible situation. On paper we had assets, we were in the red. But it was all equity and equity is totally illiquid. You cannot break off a piece of your property and take it down to the bank and ask for money. The only way to get money out of a property, other than selling, is to refinance or take out an equity line of credit. When your credit score has tanked that option really isn't available to you and even if you were to get credit, the terms would be so prohibitive, it would be just like the credit card companies had reappeared in your life, just in different form. In other words, you were trading one toxic loan for another toxic loan, not a good idea.

It was bizarre, on paper we had wealth but we could not get it. If we could not get it to pay off this staggering credit card debt, it looked to be a certainty that we stood a very good chance of losing everything. That thought alone was enough to drive me to feel physically sick over the whole ugly mess. And still, no closer to an answer.

This was without a doubt the lowest point in my life. It was about this time the debt collectors started cranking up the collection calls. At least twenty five times a day my home and cell phones would ring. I never answered, just let it go straight to voice mail. I did not want to talk to them, they were ruthless, they meant business. Or worse yet they were nice, these are the most dangerous collectors. These debt collectors wanted money and they wanted it now. As I had none to give why would I even talk to them, to feel even worse that I did? Why would I give them the chance to bully me into dipping into the mortgage to get money to them immediately, or else. These people are good and they are paid well for their very effective collection efforts.

For the most part I just ignored these calls and wouldn't answer. I wasn't just putting my head in a hole in the sand and hoping the whole mess would go away, no it dominated my every waking thought, always on that very top layer of my mind. No, I wasn't giving up, just regrouping, trying to figure a way out of this dire situation. Every once in a while I would take a call from a debt collector, just to see what they were threatening me with. Not only were they calling me but they were also calling my husband's employer. One day my daughter in law called me to give me a message to call this debt collector right away. Full of righteous indignation, I called this debt collector. "How dare you call my son," I asked, "and how did you get his phone number?" Her reply, "It is of no concern of yours how we gather our information". She must have been trained by the KGB.

They can, and they will, call your family. It is very easy to find them in this age of information. Not only that but it is legal for them to call your family as long as they do not reveal themselves to be debt collectors or tell them it is in regard to a debt. Of course if they say they are Acme Collection Agency, the cat is out of the bag. It doesn't take a genius to figure out that when someone says to your family member or friend that "It is very important that you have Leighann call us immediately at this number" they have just announced that you are a debtor who owes a debt, a deadbeat that needs to be tracked down by the likes of them.

Occasionally I would give it a whirl and try to reach some sort of resolution with a creditor. I called one creditor and made an offer to make a settlement. Her reply, "You are in no position to be calling the shots, we call the shots". OK so now you get nothing. Where do they find these people? Or do they find ordinary people and train them to be the most obnoxious, odious people on the planet? Guess what, they succeeded.

One day I opened my front door to find a piece of paper left on the porch. It was a note written on a scrap of yellow legal paper, not even the whole page, just a piece torn off. It said "Mrs. Ryan, it is in your best interest to call this number about your delinquent account". I was being stalked! Who is creeping around my house leaving threatening notes. Now this is scary. It felt like I had made a deal with the devil. The powers that the credit card companies have over the consumer are frightening. It seemed they could do just about anything and get away with it.

I thought usury was against the law. If an individual lent you money and charged 32% interest, they would be a loan shark performing an illegal act. So how do the credit card companies get away with it? What drives them? Greed, pure and simple. Unmitigated greed run amok. They have a bag of tricks and deceptive practices that would make Al Capone blush.

You know how it is when you have a problem and for the life of you, you cannot get it out of your mind? It is always right there, right in front, day and night. You focus and dwell on it almost every waking moment, it takes over your life. You may try and force yourself to think of something else to distract you. That may work for a while but eventually your mind will wander back to that problem and you will be hit anew with panic and worry. The more you try and push those thoughts out of your mind, the more stubborn they become. Your mind has a mind of its own.

Thinking maybe a change of scenery would do me good, I decided to take a little road trip and visit my best friend in upstate New York. Hopefully I could push, and keep, my worry and fear out of my mind if I was distracted by visiting with my friend. It did work too, for a while. We spent wonderful hours talking and visiting wineries, enjoying the fall foliage of the Catskill mountains. For a while my mind was cooperating and for a while, I could forget.

One night while we were sharing, what else, more wine, it all came flooding back with a vengeance. One minute we were talking and laughing and the next moment, in a hot rush, it came back, all the worry and pain that had been my constant companion for far too long. I dropped my head and didn't even try to fight the despair, I was tired of fighting it off. I felt like I could not stay another minute more, pretending, trying to forget this world of mine that was crashing down around my shoulders. The urge to get up and run out the door was overwhelming. I thought I would pretend to get an emergency call from home and needed to leave right away. The complete feeling of wretchedness made me just want to be alone. The pain was becoming too hard to bear. Fortunately I fought the panic and was able to take leave of the visit as originally planned. I had no idea who I was becoming, only that I was scaring myself.

As bad as things were at this point, I was in for a rude surprise. The one positive we had going was the fact that the apartment building was fully rented. That was good because it took all the rents coming in to pay the mortgage, line of credit and other related expenses. It was walking a tightrope for sure, but hey what else was new. As this apartment building was for the fifty five and older tenant, we marketed it as "a peaceful environment for the mature adult". We rented the last unit to a middle aged couple, the husband had serious health problems and his wife was a nurse. We signed the lease on a Friday. By Sunday I had three other tenants call me and tell me this couple was having loud all night parties. What? Did they not understand the meaning of a peaceful environment? I made a beeline to their apartment to talk to them. They seemed surprised that there had been complaints and they promised they would keep it down

But of course it was not going to be that simple. These tenants had no intention of curbing their lifestyle and the complaints continued. Now the other tenants were threatening to leave because of these people. Not only were they having loud parties every night, there was a steady stream of shady looking characters going in and out. Not a good sign. I was pretty sure there was some serious drug use going on. The neighbors could hear them talking about "cooking crack".

Now not only was my phone ringing every other minute with debt collectors calling but tenants were also calling complaining about these tenants from hell and threatening to move out because of them. I went to see the couple and told them they had to move out or I would evict them. They agreed to leave if I would give them two weeks to find another apartment. To legally evict a tenant takes about thirty days and so I agreed, believing I would get rid of them sooner giving them the two weeks than waiting for the eviction. The reason we wanted to own property for the older tenant was because theoretically at least, by the time one actually got to be an older person they would not be causing problems like this. The times they are a-changing.

I made them sign a paper agreeing to be out in two weeks. While I was not sure how well that would hold up in court, at least I wanted to have something in writing. The complaints from the other tenants continued. All I could do was reassure them that the tenants would be out in two weeks.

For the next two weeks, I just held my breath and ticked off the days on the calendar. On the date given them to be out, my husband went to the apartment to change the locks. Of course they were still there, why had I ever thought they would actually go on their own. The man started ranting and raving at my husband, his wife was in jail by this time. I jumped in my car and sped to the apartments. We went to the unit and knocked on the door. When the big oaf answered the door, I pushed past him waving the agreement in the air and asked him if he remembered signing it. He had some suspicious looking character there yelling at me that the agreement was not worth the paper it was written on. I told him to butt out, this did not concern him. The tenant got within a foot of my face and started screaming at me, my husband stepped between us and then the friend got into the huddle. It was beginning to look like a good old-fashioned throw down. Then the tenant started running around the apartment, yelling and pulling at his hair. It was apparent nothing was going to get resolved. We turned and left with the parting shot "see you in court", and cried all the way home. I just knew they were going to trash the place and we had no money to fix it. I was officially in hell.

About the same time this crisis was going on, small fissures started opening up in the asphalt parking lot that we had just put in six months before at a cost of $15,000. Everyday they grew bigger, the small fissures became large ruts. I called the paving contractor to fix the parking lot. "Not my responsibility", he replied. "It was the fault of the company that laid the base". But the paving contractor was the one who subcontracted the work to the company that laid the base. Both of them pointed the finger at the other and neither one would fix it. Not even my calls of righteous indignation and threats to sue could budge either one from making the parking lot right. In the meantime a sinkhole was opening up in our brand new parking lot, a nuisance and an eyesore at the least, a major liability at the worst. I tried to hire a lawyer to sue them, like we even have the money to pay a lawyer. Maybe some pro bono work? Not a chance. "Yeah but it is for the old people", I implored. It was sure not a good time to be me.

While trying to figure how to get new financing to pay off the credit card debt, there were people we actually knew who we owed money to. It was bad enough owing money to faceless big credit card companies but owing money to the accountant, the plumber and the electrician was quite another. Hey we know these people. Even worse, we owed back property taxes on our house.

We were well into the second year of not paying the property tax and I was scared to death of losing our home.

The last two years had taken its toll in every possible way. The local newspaper published the names of delinquent tax payers. That hurt, seeing our names in print, and wondering who else was seeing it. Definitely a cringe moment. I was carrying around far more pain than I knew what to do with.

In addition to worrying about the crushing debt, there was an on-going struggle with everyday expenses. You know how that can be. Many days would find me rummaging through old purses, pockets and couch cushions, looking for change to buy toilet paper and kitty food. One day I found $25 and felt rich. Going from managing a half million dollar construction project to couch diving really sucked.

One day there was an ad in the newspaper, "make money in your spare time delivering phonebooks, all you need is a car". I showed up at the distribution center and told them to "load me up", the more phone books delivered, the more money for me. Do you know how much 200 phonebooks weigh? After I got done paying for my new shocks and suspension system, I would make $20.

I set out with my 200 phonebooks determined to deliver them all by days' end. This however wasn't just a matter of tossing a phonebook on a porch, you had to deliver the phonebook to a specific address and you had to cross reference it on your data sheet. After about three hours and delivering about fifty phonebooks, with my car laboring along under the weight, I realized this was not one of my better ideas. This was an eight year old car with 130,000 miles on it and I was supposed to be babying it along, not loading it up with heavy phonebooks. That just shows what desperation will drive you to. People do nutty things when they are desperate. I drove back to the distribution station and told them to take all those dam phonebooks out of my car, I quit. While backing up to the loading dock for the dockhands, my car died. Just like that, it died. The phonebooks had killed it. At the exact moment the car died, the phone rang.

"Hello" I choked into the phone. It was a mortgage broker that had been looking for new financing for the apartment building. "Good news." she said, "We think we can get your financing". What? Did I hear right. One moment I was in agony over killing my car for a few bucks and someone calls me with good news for a change. While I did hear that pesky little qualifier "think", that was close enough of a yes for me. It was an immediate shift from despair to hopeful optimism in one fell swoop. She promised to get back to me when she had more information. In the meantime the dockhands helped me get my car started. "Sounds like a fuel pump", they proclaimed. How much is a fuel pump? Whatever it is, I can't afford it.

That ended my telephone delivering gig. Now the car needed a fuel pump. Doing the credit card shuffle, I found a card that still had several hundred dollars of available credit on it. The day the car was to go in for repair, my son asked me to keep my grandson and he would take my car in as the shop was next to his office. I gave him my credit card to pay for the work. When he came home he placed the invoice on the table. I glanced at it and it said, in big, bold letters, DECLINED. If I had thought before I could not possibly feel worse, I was wrong. He told me not to worry, he took care of it. I mumbled my thanks and bolted.

The phone book debacle, the throw down with the tenant from hell and my credit card being denied all happened in one hellish week.

If you are reading I am sure you can probably identify intimately with these feelings of utter despair and hopelessness. I now understood what drove some people to commit suicide. When you see no good solution of a way out, it is easy to see how many tortured souls are seduced into thinking the only way out of their hell is through their death. It was never a solution for me. I was far too infatuated with myself. A personality profile had proved without a shadow of a doubt that my personality type, an intuitive introvert, was notoriously known for being a legend in their own mind. Yep, that's me, all right. I still clung to the hope that financing might be found for the apartment complex. I would have taken almost any loan, anything to stop the hemorrhaging, and figure out later how to replace it with more favorable financing. When you are drowning, you would probably even grab a snake if you thought it could save you.

A few days later the mortgage broker called and told me she was very sorry but they could not find a lender to take our loan. A commercial investment has much stricter underwriting guidelines and we did not fit any of them. With our FICA score pretty much trashed it was all over for us. Without the new financing we could not pay off the credit card debt, not if we paid on it for the next fifty years. It was a moot point anyway as we did not have the money to even make the payments. Chances were looking better and better that we would lose everything, the house and apartments we had worked so hard for, gone.

And then it happened. An "aha" moment. In one split instant I was struck with an answer, a way out of the pain, well maybe not all the way, but a darned good start. It was the first genuine hope I had felt in a long time.

We had been talking about my husband retiring for quite a while, it was our goal. But in our present situation when we didn't even have enough money to meet our every day expenses, not even taking into consideration the credit card debt, it seemed out of the question. If we were struggling on what we were making now, how could he retire and live on less? But in that moment I remembered hearing somewhere that when you retire from the system my husband belonged to, you could opt to take a partial lump sum payment and reduce your monthly benefit and still get to keep your health benefits. I had not given it any thought since retirement seemed to be out of the question. But what if he retired and took a partial lump sum payment? We could survive on that for quite a while and it would give me some breathing room to figure out the rest. A large infusion of cash could make a huge difference in our lives. We could pay off the property taxes, the accountant, the plumber and the other miscellaneous debts we had and hopefully stave off the credit card companies until I could figure out a way to deal with them.

I asked my husband how he felt about retiring now and he asked me if I was kidding. When I told him my idea, he got very excited and of course said yes. While he had dreamed of retirement he didn't see how we could pull it off. I showed him how we could. With all his skills and experience I had no doubt he could pick up plenty of work on his own.

That was the first step out of the hell we were in. It wasn't going to solve everything but it would help greatly. There was still a long way to go in solving the credit card debt problem. The money we would be receiving from the lump payment would no where near pay off the debt. But as long as the property taxes got paid and we did not have to worry about losing our home, I had hope all the other problems could get worked out. Things were definitely looking up. For the first time in a long time, I knew peace.

CHAPTER FIVE

A FUNNY THING HAPPENED......
PART THREE

It is amazing what a little peace of mind can do. Now instead of the constant torment of despair, there was hope that just maybe it would all somehow work out. I knew I was just buying time but time is what was needed.

Finally I did find a mortgage broker who said he could get us new financing on our home but not the building. Underwriting guidelines are not as stringent on owner occupied property like they are on commercial property. I really did not like the idea of putting our home at risk but I had no choice. This was probably our last hope.

Our home would have to appraise at a high enough figure to have enough equity left after paying off the first loan and second loan. We had taken out a second loan to make the down payment on the construction loan. Appraisals can be, and often are, quite arbitrary. That is one of the major reasons the housing market and thus the whole economy has taken such a huge hit. Many appraisals in the boom years of real estate were "fudged", to say the least. The "exotic loans" were exploding. This type of financing was very popular and as long as there was the belief house prices would keep appreciating, this financing was pretty much "business as usual". A loan could be made for 125% of the value of the property. This was the perfect storm.

These loans were risky but remember the real estate market had been red hot for years and any prudence was pretty much thrown to the wind. Homeowners looked to their homes as ATM machines, a bad habit that was stripping out any equity they had, especially when they were getting loans for 100% to 125% loan to value loans. They were borrowing against equity that they didn't even yet have, and the lenders went right along. Everyone was making money and wanted to keep this hot streak going.

As if borrowing on equity you didn't even have yet were not risky enough, typically these borrowers were getting ARM loans, adjustable rate mortgages, meaning your mortgage payment could jump up hundreds of dollars. Your lender will tell you your loan will start with a low "teaser" rate then after a period of time, your loan would adjust. If your credit is shaky you may have a high interest rate to start with but when your loan resets, you will just refinance into another loan with a lower rate once you have cleaned up your "credit".

After your rate resets at a much higher interest rate, forcing your monthly payments to go up, the proverbial shit will most certainly hit the fan. When your house payment goes up hundreds of dollars, you will experience a new kind of pain.

The lender may or not tell you all of the facts. It is, of course, in the closing papers, but let's be honest, how many people do you think really read every word in the closing documents? Even if the homeowner did actually read it and understand what it really meant, the lender would hasten to assure you that when that time came, they would refinance you into a loan with lower interest. How does the broker know what the rate will be then? How does he know what rate the borrowers' credit will warrant at that time? Yes the consumer has a responsibility to know what they are getting into, but unfortunately, especially when it comes to the biggest investment you will every make, many people don't. Even if they did read it chances are good they would not understand all the terms and legalese.

So here you are, your house resets at the new rate and you cannot make the payments. I know the feeling, that is what happened when the credit card payments doubled and I couldn't pay. Before long you will find yourself at fore-closures door, a door nobody wants to be standing in front of. Multitudes of homeowners have found themselves at that door and many more will too before this whole ugly scenario plays itself out.

I met with the broker who told me he could get a new loan for our home. What he was offering was the exact same scenario just described. I told him what the house had appraised at two years ago, he said he could get an appraisal stating it was worth at least $90,000 more. He knew the figure needed to pay off credit card debt and he was working backwards to net what we needed. The interest rate would be 9% (the going rate was 6%) and it would reset at 13% in two years, but not to worry, he would just refinance me down to a lower rate.

Listening with a sinking feeling as he went over the terms of the loan, I felt very uneasy. The new loan would double our mortgage payment. Yes we would be getting the money to pay off the debts but at what price? As he pressed for me to sign the application papers, I told him I would get back to him. That night I shot up out of a sound sleep with one thought. "What the hell am I thinking?" It was a struggle now to make the mortgage payment on the house, how could we pay double? Wow, that was close. It was a certainty that we would have lost the house if we had gone through with that loan. It was one thing to risk losing an investment property and quite another to lose your home. NEVER pay off unsecured debt like credit cards and medical bills with your home. Far better to file for bankruptcy and keep your home sweet home.

It was back to the drawing board for me, I was running out of ideas.

After considering the reality of lawsuits, liens and garnishments and their imminent arrival, I started to consider bankruptcy. Like the majority of people I was pretty ignorant about bankruptcy. The myths, stigma and misinformation surrounding bankruptcy are so prevalent they appear to be taken as truths. All I knew, or thought I knew, was that it was bad. It was not about the stigma or failure that is wrongly associated with bankruptcy, my theory is that there is no failure, only opportunities for experience and growth. If you have learned anything from any experience, then it could not be a failure. I am a whiz at rationalization if nothing else. Bankruptcy carries a threatening and mystifying connotation and humans fear what they don't know or understand.

I asked my real estate attorney to recommend a good bankruptcy lawyer. You need an attorney who specializes in bankruptcy and please don't just pick one out of the phonebook. Do some research, it is well worth it. Would you go to an orthopedic doctor for a brain tumor? When you are sitting in front of the bankruptcy judge or trustee, you want to have a specialist, they will be saving your financial life. I am sure we can all agree that your financial life pretty much is your life, as finances go, so goes your life.

It was settled, we would file for bankruptcy. However when I met with the attorney, I was to find out we didn't qualify. Didn't qualify? How could that be? Apparently they have means test and we did not pass any of them, not at least if we had any hope of hanging onto everything we held dear. It was not possible that we could have come this far to fail and lose all we had slaved for, sacrificed for and loved so much.

The attorney explained there were two types of individual bankruptcies. Chapter 7 and Chapter 13. We could file a Chapter 7 and keep our house but lose the apartment building. That was no option far as I could see. What did we go through all that for if only to have to lose it? A Chapter 13 would not do either as we would be forced to sell the apartments to pay back the creditors.

Drat, that was our last card. We had wealth on paper but no money to pay the debts. Because our credit has tanked we could not qualify for new financing. What a bizarre predicament. While most people would be thrilled to have wealth on paper, it was doing us no good and was instead hindering us from getting relief through bankruptcy protection. The attorney said that most people "would kill to be in our shoes", a reference to our substantial net worth. A lot of good it was doing us though. I felt trapped in a hell of my own making. The attorney said that most likely the creditors would eventually start filing judgments and liens which could result in a loss of property.

I leaned over the desk to him and said "Do you know how they will come after us?" I was reminded of the scene in *"The Godfather"* part one when Robert Duvall leans over to Al Pacino while they were sitting in the cemetery for the burial of his father, and asks him if he knows how his enemies will come after him now that his father is gone. He said when the summons starting flying, it would be the beginning of the end. I thanked him for his time and left.

I felt deflated, reminiscent of another scene from *"The Godfather"* part one, when Robert Duvall tells Marlon Brando that his son is dead, you just saw the air go right out of him and heard a tortured sound. Yep, that was pretty much how I felt. As bad as I felt however, I also had this bizarre feeling of pride that anyone would actually "kill to be in my shoes", although at the moment they were killing me.

My mind kept bounding back and forth between hope for a resolution and facing the fact of no resolution. Lucky for me though I never stay deflated too long. "I am after all, me" as Signourney Weaver proclaims in *"Working Girl"* when she is asking Melanie Griffith, who could not get her a reservation, if Melanie had told them who it was for.

If we could not get our money out by refinancing we would have to figure out a way to make some money, make that lots of money. I still had an active real estate license. The main tool in my arsenal as a real estate agent and an investor was the MLS, the multiple listing service. This is where you can access information about any properties for sale, or that have sold, expired or withdrawn. The plan was to use the MLS to find creative real estate deals. We had never had to take that route before as financing had never been a problem. It was as easy as finding the property and going to the bank and getting the money. Remember, we used to be golden. But now that avenue was closed off and any real estate we acquired would have to be by creative financing.

I started cruising the MLS looking for creative owner financing deals as we would not be getting any loans from lenders, the tanked FICA score and all. We had started our real estate investing career investing in single family houses. Since we had built our apartment complex and saw how much easier it was, not to mention more profitable, I decided to focus strictly on apartment buildings.

I would search out the expired listings, usually the most motivated and receptive to any offer, and contact the owner to inquire if the property was still for sale. If it was, I would then make an offer on it. I would know the market value of the property, this is found in the comps. One never knows what motivates a seller and what they will ultimately agree to. The only way to find out is to put an offer out there. I started contacting all sellers that had property that had not sold and advising them of my interest in their property. This usually got me a 90% response from owners. My goal was to acquire apartment buildings on a lease option, with favorable terms of course.

One day I got a call from an owner in New Jersey that I had sent a letter of interest to. She and her husband owned several apartment buildings in our area and had been trying to sell them with no luck. They expressed an interest in my offer. Through the course of several conversations with both the woman and her husband I learned the reason they wanted to sell. They had been paying a hefty fee every month for property management and were very dissatisfied with the service.

Ding, ding, ding. My ears pricked up when I hear that, never one to miss a possible opportunity. "But Mrs. Austin, we do that too". The truth is we never worked for anyone else managing property but we had our own rental properties for ten years, so that qualified us. I just didn't mention we never did it for anyone else. Experience is experience. I told her we had been managing property for ten years and my husband had twenty years experience in property maintenance, which he had. Not only did we have experience, we were property owners ourselves and could appreciate the significance of good property management. I was excited now. I told her I would put together a proposal but that if we could not come to terms on the lease-option, perhaps they would consider us to be their new property management company. My husband was getting set to retire from his "real" job soon and we could step right into our new property management gig.

This was a great idea I had never even thought of. We could start our own property management company. We were perfectly positioned for this business endeavor. We would be so much more than just the maintenance man that unclogged the toilet and the landlady that just collected the rent. We would be Real Estate Investment Asset Managers. Sounds better, don't you think?

Shortly after my husband retired, I got a call from Mrs. Austin. They decided they could not meet the terms offered to lease option the properties but they would be very happy if we would take over the job of property management. THEY would be happy?

We set up our business, got incorporated, printed letterhead and cards and we were in business. Another bonus for us was that the previous management company had done such a poor job, many of the units needed to be rehabbed. Yes, we did that too. So in addition to our management fee, we also made money rehabbing the units. The tide was starting to turn for us. My plan didn't work out exactly as hoped for, we didn't acquire the property but we did acquire a new career.

Now that we had more money coming in, I started calling up all our creditors, all fifteen of them, to try and work out a repayment plan. Some were agreeable, some were not. Some wanted their money now, all of it. Two of the creditors agreed to a lump sum, which was going to come out of our lump sum payment. By the time I had worked through all fifteen, I had settled two accounts and set up repayment plans on five. That left eight accounts I still had to worry about.

However I made a huge mistake. When setting up the repayment accounts, the creditors insisted it had to be done electronically, you had to give them your checking or savings account number. Foolishly, I did. Don't you make the same mistake. If a creditor tells you it has to be set up electronically, tell them no. Once you have given them electronic access, they can clean out your accounts.

If the mail service is not good enough for them, too bad. I went to five different banks and set up five different accounts for each of the repayment plans and only deposited every month the agreed upon amount. I knew enough to not be totally comfortable with the creditors having access to my account so I was hedging my bets. The most they could get out of the account every month was that amount, and no more.

As the months went on, some debt collectors that I had not been able to reach agreements with dropped out of the race and some tenaciously hung on, like pit bulls on steroids. Some had moved on from calling, they were now filing lawsuits. It was a given that the summons would not be far behind. Living in the country, very few people just showed up at our door. If someone did come knocking, I was sure it was someone after us. Paranoia reigned supreme. I pictured them with a bullhorn, telling me the house was surrounded, and to come out with my hands up. Of course I would never answer the door, I figured if they can't find me, they can't serve me.

If I saw a strange car pull into the driveway I would hurry into the basement and shut the door so I would not have to hear them beating on the door. Once when hurrying down the steps I slipped and almost fell down the stairs. What was wrong with me, I could have broken my fool neck. Served me right, hiding like a thief. I did not want to go through life looking over my shoulder, I wanted closure. But I had no idea how to get it.

One debt collector called me to read me my Miranda rights. Was he kidding? Just one of the many rotten tricks debt collectors pull on someone when they are at their most vulnerable. While I would be the first to admit it is not good to be a debtor, it is by no means a criminal act. There are many frightened people, so beat up, and down, who would have fell for that.

As a survivor of bankruptcy, I do want to add that while being a debtor is not a crime, ignoring any correspondence from the courts could be grounds for them to issue a warrant for your arrest for contempt of court. Always respond to any correspondence from the court, it usually means a lawsuit has been filed against you and it also means the time for some response and action is at hand. In other words, don't panic until you hear from the court.

My day to panic arrived. A letter from the court arrived ordering my husband to appear in court as he was being sued. Yes, I opened his mail, in case you were wondering. Since I handled all things financial anyway, he was on a need to know basis. And so far he did not need to know. This summons changed the game. As this card was in his name, he was the one who would have to appear in court. Just like in the old *"I Love Lucy"* series I would have some "splaining to do".

The really interesting thing about this lawsuit was this was from a creditor that we owed the smallest amount to and it was the last one defaulted on. OK, this is my test case. I called the lawyer representing the creditor. He talked to me even though I was not on the account, they just wanted their money. I agreed to a repayment plan and the suit was dismissed, just like that.

Well that wasn't so bad. However I knew we could not absorb a lot more of these plans, especially since most of the other creditors were owed much larger sums of money. I was sure they would not settle for $200 a month on a debt of say, oh $10,000 or $25,000.

It was about that same time that we got charged with a 4th degree misdemeanor. To date I had gotten through life with no more than a speeding ticket. We still had two of the original houses that we had bought that we were using as rentals. One was paying for itself and we had planned to hold onto that one. The other house had been a good investment but the neighborhood had deteriorated and it was getting harder to find a tenant, one that would actually pay the rent.

As the neighborhood had deteriorated, so had the house. We tried our best to keep up with it through the years but as our financial situation had worsened, so had our ability to keep up with the needed repairs. When the last tenant had moved out and pretty much trashed the place, we could not keep up the mortgage payments nor could we bring the house back to rentable condition. We couldn't feed it, we could not sell it for what was owed and we could not get a tenant, at least not one who would actually pay the rent. By this time the only tenants who would live in that neighborhood were drug addicts and criminals.

We did the only thing we could do, we let it go back to the bank. In the meantime the city slapped us with a housing code violation due to the condition of the house. The city did not care that we did not have the money to bring it up to code or that we were losing it in foreclosure. We were given a summons to appear in court.

We showed up on the assigned day and checked in with the bailiff. We were told to go into a certain courtroom. We took our seats and the proceedings got underway. As the other people in the room were called and their charges read, I began to think there had been a mistake and we were sent to the wrong courtroom. These people were here for DUI, drug dealing, drug possession, stalking, theft and assault. I thought, wait a minute, we don't belong here with these criminals, we were simply here for a housing code violation. We were not drug dealers or thieves, just hardworking individuals that fell upon some hard times and cannot afford to bring our rental property up to code. My husband finally leaned over and said "I don't think we belong here".

I left the courtroom and went to find the bailiff to inform him he had sent us to the wrong courtroom, we were here merely for a housing code violation. I told him our name, he scanned the roster and said "no mistake, you belong there, go back and sit down". I slunk back to my seat and told my husband, that yes indeed, we did belong here.

When our names were called to go before the judge, he simply said that we needed to comply or he would put us in jail. As I never thought I looked good in stripes, we told him we would find a way to comply, lucky for us he gave us a couple months to make the needed repairs. Shortly after, the house went into foreclosure. At some level I did worry about the lender coming after us with a deficiency judgment in the future, but can't worry about that, I have enough creditors after us right now, in the present.

Finally we got our lump sum settlement. What a feeling of relief. There is something that borders on a spiritual experience when you get to clear bills off your desk. The best feeling of all was paying off the back property taxes on our home. We had money coming in from our property management and rehab business and that eased our financial situation greatly. All the units in the apartment building were rented and finally that investment was feeding itself. We patched the sinkhole in the parking lot and evicted the middle aged delinquents from hell. While I was convinced that they would trash the place, all it needed was a paint job. Life's looking pretty good again.

Yes it was still an on-going battle with the credit card companies and collection agencies I had not been able to negotiate with. They wanted it all and they wanted it now. And so it went, they would constantly call and I would constantly blow them off. Every so often I had the urge to really get into it with them but I feared that would be like waving a red flag in front of a bull, they would just become more aggressive and menacing. Human nature being as it is, I was sure they would just make an extra effort to cause me grief. I had to be smarter than them, that shouldn't be too hard to do. Besides, calls could not hurt me, I was not going to panic until more summons start arriving.

OK, it is now time to panic again. Apparently my statute of limitations was up with the various collectors as now the summons were coming fast and furious. This I could not ignore. The day of reckoning would soon be upon us. There would be no defense when it went to court. The creditor would of course win a judgment and a lien would be filed against us and our property. I knew there was no possible way of reaching a prepayment plan that we could actually afford, not with the balances so high. It would take thousands each month just to satisfy them all, never mind about ever, ever getting them paid off.

In desperation I called the bankruptcy attorney I had talked to the previous year and told him about the pending lawsuits. He advised me that depending on how much was owed and how much we owned, the creditors could request the court to force a sale of our properties. Since we owed huge amounts, I knew it was going to get ugly. I was sure they would force the sale of our properties. There was no way out. It looked like a certainty that we were going to lose everything we had worked so hard for and sacrificed so much. Our house, gone. Our apartment building, gone.

Sometime into the conversation I once again inquired about getting a bankruptcy. He said, with a slight exasperation in his voice, that we did not qualify to file bankruptcy and keep our properties as we had too much equity. But wait, it has been well over a year since that conversation. Real estate values had fallen greatly and our equity had been reduced as a result. With the first and second mortgages against both our home and apartment building we are now underwater on both properties. We also owed two years of property taxes on the apartment building. The bottom line was more was owed than could be cleared in a sale. Given these new developments and a new set of circumstances, wouldn't we now be eligible for a Chapter 13. The attorney fell silent for a couple minutes, digesting what I had just asked. After what seemed like an eternity he agreed that it could work, we could petition for our Chapter 13. Whoever would have thought plunging property values and back property taxes would be a blessing.

It is impossible to describe that moment of relief and joy. We could have a Chapter 13 bankruptcy and get to keep everything. After the years of worry, stress, despair and pain, it was soon going to be over. What a resolution it was too, not only would it be over, we would still have our precious home and apartments.

A Chapter 13 involves a repayment plan, of sorts. The court sets up a repayment plan which you pay into every month. It is a set amount based on information that you give them. The amount you pay back is not the amount you owe. If you owed $100,000 in debt, you could conceivably pay back only $100 a month, and no not for life. The plan is for three to five years. If your plan was for five years, at $100 a month, you would pay back $6000 of your $100,000 debt. I had to fill out a packet of papers as thick as a small town phone book. Some might say the questionnaire is intrusive. I say, get real. You are asking for protection from the court from your creditors. There are legions of debt collectors out there who know plenty about you already, why would you care what the court knows. I would rather have the law on my side protecting me than have the creditors using the law to persecute me.

Be prepared for the paperwork you must complete when filing. After what you have been through, a little paperwork is a piece of cake. The court determines how much you pay into your bankruptcy plan based on what your disposable income is. The key to the puzzle in a Chapter 13 bankruptcy is the Expense Schedule. This will list all your expenses. The following is a list of expenses they will ask you about.

Rent or Mortgage

Real Estate Taxes (if not included in the mortgage)

Insurance (if not included in your mortgage)

Utilities, electricity and heating fuel

Water and sewer

Telephone

Cable

Other (types of utilities)

Home maintenance

Food

Clothing

Laundry and dry cleaning
Medical and dental expenses (not covered by insurance)
Transportation (not including car payments)
Children's activities
Recreation
Entertainment
Newspapers
Magazines, etc.
Charitable contributions
Insurance - Homeowners or renters
Insurance - Life
Insurance - Health
Insurance - Auto
Insurance - other
Taxes (not deducted from wages)
Installment payments
Auto (total of all auto loans)
Other installment loans
Alimony, maintenance and support to others
Payments for support of additional dependents
not living in your home
Professional expenses

Did you notice items like cable, recreation, and entertainment? How about children's activities? This doesn't really seem like deprivation to me, the court is not interested in punishing you with an impoverished lifestyle. This questionnaire does not require you to document anything, they need no proof of what you pay for food. You then add up all your expenses and subtract them from your income. This is your disposable income, the amount you will pay every month into your repayment plan for the next three to five years.

The monthly payment into the plan would turn out to be a mere fraction of the monthly payments that we would have paid to the creditors with never an end in sight. Now we had an end in sight. Without benefit of bankruptcy, we would have been paying until we died and dodging collectors and lawsuits.

The day came when I had to tell my husband we were filing bankruptcy. The jig was up. It had never occurred to me when we started this project it would end up like this. I envisioned us going on to build many more units for the elderly and handicapped. With a bankruptcy we wouldn't be able to do that any time soon, if ever. In retrospect it is evident that we wouldn't be in this position if so many things had not happened differently. But it is what it is.

I don't want to sound like the people who smoke for thirty years then blame the tobacco industry because they got cancer. But facts are facts, if they had not tripled my interest rate where I could not pay the minimum, which caused the default, which led to the inability to get new financing, this wouldn't have happened. It was pure unadulterated greed on their part. I know they are in business to make money and they have been making billions off the public for years.

So back to telling the husband. I would put the most positive spin on this news as possible. When he came home from work one night I told him we had to talk, a declaration that makes most spouses cringe. I told him that after careful consideration and soul searching, (and threats and lawsuits), I thought that the best possible course of action for us was to file bankruptcy and that I needed his signature, sign here, press hard.

Now I realize that this scenario would probably not play out among many couples. As finances are the single biggest subject couples fight about, it is a given that if there is a conversation taking place about money, there will be fights and blame a-plenty.

We turned in the necessary paperwork to the attorney and he prepared it for submission for our petition. Both my husband and I had to take mandatory credit counseling and submit the certificate. We took it online at a cost of $70 for the both of us. Then we had to both talk to a credit counselor on the phone. We talked about budgeting issues and if we understood how we had gotten into a difficult financial situation. It was all very pleasant and helpful, not judgmental in the least.

When the petition papers were ready we went to the attorney's office to sign them and the petition was submitted to the bankruptcy court. The day it was submitted it was like a security blanket dropping over us. The harassing phone calls stopped dead. The correspondence from creditors and summons from courts stopped immediately. This is called an "automatic stay". I felt like Teflon. It is very difficult to describe the feeling but I'll try. I felt like someone who had a terminal illness and as they lay dying, a miracle cure was found for them. They got their life back. I am not trying to equate our debt problem with someone who is dying, it is just an analogy, one that describes my feelings perfectly. No more fearing the phone and the mailbox, no hiding behind the drapes when someone comes to my door, and no more worrying that we would lose everything we had worked so hard and long for and end up living in our car, if we even had a car.

It was a new day. Finally now we could look towards the future, knowing now that we had a future. When you are drowning in debt you feel like you will never again be able to buy anything or go anywhere. It felt like all the material things in life would be forever out of reach. Not only would the material be out of reach, peace of mind would be unattainable. If we were to try and pay back all our creditors we would have been like those old people you hear about eating dog food. Now I knew that was not to be our fate. Never again would we be slaves to the credit card companies, sending them money into a black hole and never getting the debt monkey off our back. Now we were going to be free.

Now all that was left to do was wait for our "meeting of the creditors" the 341 meeting. This is where all the creditors we owed would have the opportunity to confront us. Not looking forward to that at all. My attorney assured me the creditors never actually attended these meetings. "Oh they will attend ours" I told him. I was sure that since we owed so many, and so much, they would make an exception in our case and show just to get a look at us. I was positive we would need a big room just to hold them all. Little did I realize how insignificant we were to them. We were just an account number, one who owed them money, but just a number none the less. It is a truth that when we are facing adversity we believe we are the only ones doing so, we must get over this and realize that many people before and so many people after us will walk the same path. It helps to take the sting out of a situation if you will only realize that you are so not alone, and that you will not only survive but come out in a far better place.

The 341 meeting would be the first and possibly only meeting with the bankruptcy trustee and the creditors. Despite what my attorney said, I was sure our many creditors would be there. There was a two month wait between the filing and the 341 meeting. While I did have some anxiety about this meeting I assured my husband that it was just routine, no big deal.

Finally the day of the meeting arrived. Your case is filed with the bankruptcy district that serves your particular county. We had to go to a town about ninety miles away. We thought it would take about two hours to get there, so we allowed for four. It would not do to be late for your bankruptcy meeting. On the trip there I was filled with apprehension and a bundle of nerves. I had our story ready as to why poor us had gotten into this predicament. I had an urge to purge. I wanted to be certain the powers that be and who would be ruling on our petition understood what brought us to their court this early summer day.

My expectation was of a serious looking, austere courtroom, sitting there in a witness chair and being grilled like they might do in a Jimmy Cagney movie. When we pulled up in front of the address the attorney had given me, my first thought was there must be a mistake. But no, it was the right address. It was an old, slightly seedy office building. Not too intimidating. When we got off the elevator, we found ourselves actually waiting in line to check in with the receptionist. There must have been thirty other people there. This put me immediately at ease. There is comfort in knowing there are many other people in the same boat as you.

We sat out in the hallway and waited to be called. We would watch the others go into that inner office with their lawyer and then soon we would watch them walk out. How bad can this be? It is only taking twenty five minutes and they all look pretty good when they come out. Nobody is crying or appears upset. Whatever is going on in that office, it will be over in a short time.

Our name was called and we and our attorney went into the room. It was just a plain old everyday office. There was a large desk and two women were sitting behind it. We were instructed to sit down, raise our hand and swear to tell the truth and talk into the microphone. One of the women was the trustee and the other was her assistant. They asked us basic questions like our name and address. They asked if everything was true on our petition to the best of our knowledge. The trustee addressed some questions to our lawyer and the meeting was over. The trustee recommended making two amendments to our petition and she set a date to return in 2 months. We weren't even required to attend this confirmation, just our attorney was. And just like that, it was over.

CHAPTER SIX

THAT PESKY MORALITY QUESTION

So how do we respond to the questions of the morality of bankruptcy? Or is it even a question, or a concern? Some people considering may worry about the ethics of walking away from all or a good portion of their debt.

Morality is defined in the dictionary as

1. Accepted moral standards
2. How right and wrong something is as defined by moral standards

But who sets the standards and what is considered right and what is considered wrong?

The Pilgrims who lived in Salem during the early part of our country's history might be considered to be prim and proper "moral" God-fearing people but they burned people at the stake they perceived to be witches. How do you think that set with their God?

The Romans entertained themselves pitting man and beast against each other to the death. In one day alone 50,000 humans and animals were killed as sport and entertainment.

In Africa today there are still tribes that allow for a male member of a family to kill his sister if she disgraces the family name.

A man may stone his wife to death in the middle east in this day and age and it is acceptable in their culture.

I could cite examples all day but you get the picture. None of these four examples seem moral to me. Morality is subjective. What is moral for one person, one culture, one time does not make it moral for all persons, all cultures or for all time.

Do I feel bad, ashamed, irresponsible or immoral being among the hundreds of thousands that filed in one year alone? The answer is an unequivocal and resounding "No". Do you want to know how I really feel? Like a survivor.

I feel like I have been given not a stay of execution to spend the rest of my life in prison but have instead been given the keys to the prison gates. In a word, freedom.

Consider this. When you opt for bankruptcy, you are choosing that over destitution. To be sure there are many who foolishly live a life of over consumption far beyond their means with nary a thought how they are going to pay for it. But the majority of people filing bankruptcy are doing so because of forces beyond their control. The cost of living, death in the family, job loss, illness and accident, inadequate or no health care, divorce and a host of other contributors make the cost of living, well let's just say we can hardly afford to live.

When the costs of necessities like housing, food, clothes, gas, health care, education and cars rise faster than our income, what do we do? We put it on plastic. Some even pay their mortgages on plastic. How many times have we used plastic because we did not have the money?

It used to be that the majority of bankruptcies occurred because of unexpected life events. Today it is just as likely that people will face bankruptcy because they have been using plastic to get by on. They have been spending more than they take in and you can only do that for so long before it all ends, badly.

The housing market crash has been a major factor in the increase in bankruptcy filings. People would pull out their equity by a refinance or equity line of credit, more often than not inflated equity, to pull their chestnuts out of the fire. The combination of declining home values and the credit freeze has put a lock on that piggy bank.

Did the homeowner have a responsibility not to squander their equity? Yes, they did. But it is human nature to think that the good times are going to last, that their property will just keep appreciating. Isn't that what the pundits and economists tell us? Given the fact that the United States' economy is no longer backed by gold but by consumer confidence, isn't it our patriotic duty to believe that the party will last forever?

Surprise!

Many who will lay a moral judgment on a person filing for bankruptcy protection are doing so out of their own self-interest, certainly not yours. They have their own agenda to push. I was listening to a financial "guru" on his radio talk show one day when a gentleman called in looking for advice. He said he was 62 years old and was buried under a mountain of credit card debt and was considering filing for bankruptcy and he asked the "guru" what he thought. The gentleman was torn between struggling to pay his debts and worrying about how he would survive in his rapidly approaching older years. He was sick with worry about being old and penniless and wanted to put money into his retirement but he could not do that and pay off his staggering debts too.

The "guru" told the gentleman he had a moral responsibility to pay off his debts and as far as his worries about surviving in his later years, that was just secondary. His answer stunned me. This man had called seeking help, and he gets a smug self-serving answer. This "guru" had his own agenda, he had built an empire on the premise that, no matter what, you need to pay off your credit card debt. However that is not always in the debtors best interest to do so. But that flies in the face of the "guru's" philosophy, not to mention the sales of his books and instructional materials. The real irony is that this "guru" himself had a bankruptcy and went on to become wildly successful.

Who else might try to lay a moral judgment on you? Consider the following article published in the Christian Science Monitor, July 3, 2006 by author G. Jeffrey McDonald:

With more people buried in debt, Christians argue over forgiveness versus responsibility. Consumers daunted by mountains of debt face another uphill climb as they sort through mixed messages on the moral implications of filing for bankruptcy.

One side, Christian conservatives who applauded last year's tightening of bankruptcy laws are now appealing to a higher authority to tweak the consciences of would-be defaulters. On the other side, voices irked by double-digit interest rates and questionable marketing tactics of credit-card issuers say debtors are often morally justified in seeking relief.

The morality debate is heating up amid signs of trouble for people living on the margins:

*Even though tougher filing laws took effect October 17, 2005, the number of monthly bankruptcy filings grew by more than 300 percent between November and March, from 13,758 to 49,977, according to a June 2006 report from the Administrative Office of the U.S. Courts.

*Foreclosures on home mortgages were up 38 percent nationally in the first quarter of 2006, according to property tracker Realty Trac Inc.

*The average American household owes more than $9,300 on credit cards, up from $2,966 in 1990, according to Cardweb.com

Against this backdrop, advocates for and against the use of bankruptcy disagree about where to lay the blame when someone gets buried in debt. Christian personal finance guru Mary Hunt has a stern message for anyone considering bankruptcy, "It's absolutely legal, but it is not moral". "I would say, 'You accepted these credit cards. You had the obligation to know what you were getting into,' " says Ms. Hunt, author of "Living Your Life For Half The Price". "You spent the money, and sure you had a big medical bill, but it probably would not have put you over the edge had you not already been deeply in debt.' "

To make this case, bankruptcy's critics often cite Psalm 37:21 "The wicked borrow and do not repay, but the righteous give generously." From sources such as Crown Financial Ministries and Dave Ramsey's nationally syndicated radio show, advice seekers hear they have a duty in most cases to keep their payback promises even when life throws them a curve ball.

But another school of thought sees a more complex picture in which lenders also face admonitions to forgive debts. For instance, Jonathan Alger, a bankruptcy attorney in Orlando Fla. reminds distraught clients the American legal tradition for allowing for bankruptcy stems from Deuteronomy 15:1-11, which calls for debt forgiveness every seven years. Others agree with Mr. Alper that those who are able should repay, but those unable to do so should not feel guilty.

In Psalm 37, "the psalmist is talking about (cases where) borrowing money and not repaying it becomes a business strategy." says Gay Moore, a Christian investment adviser in Sarasota, Fla. By contrast, he says, single women should not worry about declaring bankruptcy, for instance, after using credit cards to feed their children.

"These people ought to go to bed every night knowing that God has granted them debt relief." Moore says "And they're not, because they hear this garbage (from anti-debt Christians). That's what Jesus called placing heavy burdens on his flock."

"May", a Virginian who requested anonymity to protect her reputation, knows the moral struggle well.

For fourteen years, she paid the minimum balance due until she maxed out her credit cards on routine purchases such as shoes, clothes, haircuts, gifts and equipment for her dog-grooming business. Charges initially worth $5000 resulted in a balance of $10,000, even after she increased her payment to $150 per month. Every day, she hid the mail before her husband could see her predicament, and she remembers wishing "I could go to sleep and not wake up". Yet she kept paying back her debts at close to 20 percent interest. "I did think, I did sign up for the credit card, I used it, I have a moral obligation to pay this," May says. "If I didn't feel some moral obligation, I would have told these debt collectors to take a hike." But after a creditor told her she was incurring debt faster than she could pay it down, she spoke to a lawyer, divulged her secret to her husband, and sought protection under Chapter 7. "I must have paid (creditors) way over $20,000 for a $5000 debt," May says. "Knowing in my heart that I paid everybody that I owed the original amount plus a reasonable amount of interest, I don't feel any guilt about having filed bankruptcy. I wish I had done it a lot sooner."

In Hunt's view, what matters in resolving the moral quandary is whether the borrower lived up to his or her original promise. But Alper begs to differ because, he says, the circumstances surrounding the original loan are sometimes suspect to a degree that they nullify a borrower's moral duty to repay.

"The people (whom creditors) often solicit are high-risk customers" with considerable vulnerabilities, Alper says. "By contract, they owe the money. But what's the validity of offering a lollipop to a diabetic? Or offering a cigarette to someone who's addicted to nicotine? You're not on an equal footing", and therefore the contract isn't moral in the first place, in his view.

Others might bear some blame as well, according to David Jones, president of the 177 member Association Of Independent Consumer Credit Counseling Agencies. He sees bankruptcy as morally justified in situations stemming from uncontrollable events, such as a job loss or medical emergency. But he also blames teachers and school administrators for failing to make credit education a part of most curricula. "Society has failed many people because (it) hasn't provided the kind of education and help and background that they need," Mr. Jones says. "I suppose you could say (some profligate spenders) are somewhat off the hook, but I'm a little bit concerned about that because there is a responsibility to be a good financial steward."

In Hunt's view, individuals benefit far more in the long run from belt-tightening disciplines, such as those she employed to pay non mortgage debts in excess of $100,000, than they do by filing for bankruptcy. "There's a good feeling we get when we're paying back debt," Hunt says. "Bankruptcy is the opposite of that".

But if restoring good credit is the goal, Jones has some bad news for Hunt's theory of thrifty virtue. Creditors like to see a recent history, he says, because it usually means an applicant has poor spending habits, has no debts, and is ineligible for bankruptcy for another five to seven years. In short, this applicant stands to be a near-term cash cow for the creditor."

May's experience suggests he might be right. She received three credit-card offers - including one from a previous creditor - during one week in June. "Somebody that has a lot of debt and is paying their debt and straining every month to do so is not nearly as good a credit risk as someone who has just walked out of bankruptcy," Jones says. "I would hate to invite people into bankruptcy with that scenario, but that happens to be the fact," he concludes.

Let's for a minute address the morality question not to the debtor but to the credit card companies. Creditors actually love to extend credit to people who have had bankruptcies, even very recent ones. Why? They know that the consumer cannot file again for several years and they will have them on the hook. Jackpot! The credit card companies know a cash cow when they see one.

Think about that, credit card issuers will rush to mail you credit applications AFTER you file for bankruptcy. I can attest to that, I too received offers through the mail and e-mail after filing, and still do to this day, one was actually from a creditor that was included in the bankruptcy. Bizarre. Kind of stands that question of morality on its' head.

While the credit card companies lament the losses from bankruptcy filings, they fail to admit they made billions off these very same customers who have now filed for bankruptcy. Many of the bankrupted have been paying for years and years on the account. The banks still made huge profits even though debtors were getting their debts discharged. The credit card companies will actually make more money off those who eventually file for bankruptcy than they will from their customers who pay as promised. But not to play favorites, the banks will also continue to over charge the "good" customers.

The banking industry loves their credit cards. They get four times the rate of return on credit card usage than they do on all other types of financial activity. Credit card profits are huge, if the customer is gouged, oh well. Why do they do it; because they can. The hapless consumer is no match for the credit card companies and their powerful allies, the banking lobbyists. And to be fair, the consumer is all too often a willing participant in their own "death by credit card".

What is my point? The consumer should not be made to feel ashamed or embarrassed that they found themself in a position of drowning, literally drowning, in debt I know the feeling, so do you if you are reading this. We certainly had help getting into this situation. We should accept our share of the responsibility but we should in no way feel that we committed a crime, even if the debt collectors treat you as if you had.

Starla Darling was an employee of the Archway Cooky factory in Mansfield, Ohio. She went on maternity leave on October 1, two days before the plant abruptly closed. On October 4 she got a certified letter stating that as of October 6, she would no longer have health insurance. If her baby was not born by then she would have no medical insurance to pay for the delivery. Hoping to head off this catastrophe, she implored the doctor to induce her the next day so that she could deliver before her insurance expired. After being induced and failing to deliver, the doctors were about to send her home when she began hemorrhaging. The placenta has torn away from the baby and the wall of the uterus. She was rushed into emergency surgery and the baby was delivered by caesarean section. The doctors had no time to administer pain medications before cutting into her.

After going through that nightmare, Starla found out that her health insurance had already expired. Archway had stopped paying its' part for employee health insurance months prior, causing the policies to lapse.

It would appear that businesses can, and do, pretty much whatever they can get away with and probably don't spend a lot of time wrestling with the "morality" issue. So why should you? Individuals should not be made to feel bad or worthless because they got into a situation where they were not able to keep up. Most people don't set out to deliberately default on their obligations. Yes of course there will always be some people that will run up debts with no intention of paying them, but those people are very much in the minority.

If you are still talking to your creditors and bill collectors, do not let them tell you it is your moral obligation to pay your debts. It is not immoral to not pay your debts if you truly cannot pay them. The only "moral" obligation you have is to take care of your family and yourself, and that does not mean taking food out of your families' mouths to send to your creditors. Now that would be immoral. Nor does it mean that you should raid your kid's college fund and your retirement fund to pay your creditors. That is not only wrong, it is foolish.

Never trade your non-secured debt (credit card debt, personal loans, medical bills) for secured debt (mortgage debt). Homeowners have routinely tapped their equity every chance they could to pay off credit card debt. The problem with that is, more often than not, that they would just run them up again. That can only work for so long. Refinancing your home or taking out a line of credit is risky, you stand a good chance of losing all that you hold precious, worth far more than whatever it is you charged put together. Often times it is hard to remember exactly what the debt bought.

Do not feel bad about not paying your creditors for unsecured debt. When that creditor gave you that credit card, they were taking a risk that you may not pay it back. Have you ever taken a risk and it did not work out as you had planned? Don't spend any time feeling sorry for the banks; they have been making an obscene fortune off their high interest credit cards for years. You and every other credit card holder in the world who used credit cards have been paying high interest on your credit cards for a very long time. Even with consumers defaulting in record numbers, the banks have, and still do, make a killing.

I urge you not to believe that filing for bankruptcy is immoral in any shape or form as it is not. Many people drowning in debt are too paralyzed with fear and ignorance about what bankruptcy really is and what it is meant to be. They stubbornly refuse to consider bankruptcy as it is, to them, a failure. They will eat tuna and mac and cheese for the rest of their life if they have to but they will not accept a perfectly legitimate and acceptable remedy like bankruptcy.

For these people I would offer this advice. Save yourself. If not yourself, what about your family? Bankruptcy is meant to be a fresh start. Don't you want to keep your home and your retirement money? Don't you want to be able to educate your children? Do you want to live your golden years in poverty? Don't you want a second chance? Bankruptcy will give you all that. I'm not suggesting everyone with credit card debt should rush out and file bankruptcy. If your debt is manageable and you can conceivably pay if off that is what you should do.

Bankruptcy holds our lives together and keeps us functioning. It is meant to be restorative, not just for the individual but for the whole economy. We all deserve a second chance. What will you do with yours?

CHAPTER SEVEN

BE AFRAID, BE VERY AFRAID

So spoke Geena Davis to a young girl in the company of Jeff Goldblum, a mad scientist turned into a common housefly in the movie "*The Fly*". Be very afraid of debt collectors. I will concede many debt collectors are just hard working people struggling to make a living, however that is all I will concede. It is the perfect job for anyone who loves to scare, intimidate and harass another person, and get paid for it. It is a stressful job and the turnover rate is very high. By far the most dangerous debt collector is the one who is nice to you and appears to empathize with your plight. They want you to let your guard down. They can be stealthy and would make good undercover agents. What they want from you is information. They may ask you if you have any assets you can sell to raise money to pay your debt. If you tell them about your boat, RV, motorcycle or rare coin collection, they will know you are worth pursuing.

They may talk to you as if they were talking to a friend and encourage you to confide in them. They are merely gathering information to use against you, make no mistake. They know you are vulnerable and will try to get you to confide in them, all the while trying to figure out how to extract any money they can get out of you. With a rude and harassing collector you know right where you stand and you are less likely to let your guard down.

You need not waste any time telling the collector your sob story, they really don't care, except to use the information against you. They just assume you are lying. Of course it is fine when they lie. In fairness, I am sure that there are collectors who are decent human beings and would not resort to trickery or lying. But you don't know if you are talking to one or not. In your best interest, believe that the disembodied voice on the other end belongs to a person whose sole purpose in life it to get money out of you, one way or the other. Collectors are trained to accomplish one goal, to collect the debt. They are well trained in doing whatever it takes. One particularly snarky collector told a little girl who answered the phone that they were coming to her house to take her toys because her mommy did not pay her debts. Another debt collector told a debtor that they were sending the police to their house to arrest them. Sadly, there are people vulnerable and scared enough to believe these cretins.

If you are trying to negotiate a lump settlement and they ask you where the money will come from, do not tell them under any circumstances. That is not their business, it is just another way of trying to find out about your finances.

A collector is trying to gauge whether you are worth going after. If they think you have assets, they will ratchet up their efforts to relieve you of them. They may ask you how much your house is worth and how much equity you have in it. Remember they will probably have a copy of your credit report in front of them that states how much you owe your lender on your mortgage. Let's assume your credit report says you owe $175,000 on your first and $30,000 on an equity line of credit. You owe $205,000 on the house. They ask you what you think it is worth. You say $255,000. Ding, ding, ding, they now know you have about $50,000 in equity and you are worth going after.

They could and most likely will file a judgment against you. You do not want a judgment, more on that later. They will ask you about stocks, bonds, pensions, annuities and any other income you may have. Tell them nothing. Do not tell them where you work, where your spouse works, or where you bank and most certainly not your account information. They may tell you the only way they can work with you is for you to grant them electronic access to your money in your bank. That should be a red neon light. You're giving a perfect stranger on the phone your bank account numbers. Take it from someone who made that mistake, me. If they want the money that bad they can just get it through the postal service. Once they have your account information, they can clean you out, and they do. The more you talk, the more you lose.

How many times have we heard about a scam where a person gets a call, email or letter stating that they have won something or someone died and left them money? You may get a call from Nigeria telling you that you won money but in order for you to get the money you must send them money for "processing" or some such nonsense. They could say that they need your bank account numbers so they may wire the money to you. The incredulous truth is that people give this information to a total stranger on the phone. There must be hundreds of these types of scams. You may think you would never fall for that ploy, but what do you think you are doing when you give out that information to a debt collector? Both have one object, to relieve you of your money.

While researching my options on how to deal with our debt problems, I learned that if you negotiate a settlement with the creditor, get in in writing before you send them any money. I agreed to a partial settlement with one credit card company debt collector and requested the settlement in writing. They sent me a document with the agreed upon terms and they withdrew that amount from my account. Much to my utter shock and dismay, I received a statement, an ordinary statement just like you get in the mail every month. It acknowledged the electronic payment, the one what was supposed to be a final payment settling the account. But wait, there must be some mistake, they were still billing me for the difference. I thought I had covered myself by getting it in writing, but surprise! DO NOT BELIEVE A DEBT COLLECTOR. Just go by the assumption that if their lips are moving, they are probably lying.

If you think debt collectors are shady, suspicious characters just barely operating on the right side of the law, be aware that Wall Street investors are players in this collection game. Given the recent state of affairs in the world economy stemming in large part from the Wall Street debacle, that should probably come as no surprise. It might be very hard to distinguish the dubious collectors from Wall Street, they may very well be one and the same.

You may want to pay on an old debt. Maybe you feel if you try to pay something, you will not feel so bad about your debt sin. If you do pay something, you could be making more trouble for yourself. The collector thinks if you are willing to pay some, maybe they can get you to pay more. Then you start getting into the area of diminishing returns, once you start paying you are afraid to stop, as if what you have been paying is for naught if you stop. That is what the collectors are hoping for. Pavlov would be proud. When you pay an old debt you also restart the seven year statute of limitations.

If you do settle your account for less than what you owe on it, that money is reported to the IRS and you owe taxes on the money forgiven, the amount not repaid. You owe Visa $9000 and settle for $3000, the credit card company "lost" $6000. They report it to the IRS as income to you, you "saved" it by not paying it, or as the IRS sees it, you "earned" $6000. You will now pay tax on it as it is income. If you are in the 28% income bracket you would pay a tax of $1680 on the money that was "forgiven". If you or your accountant do not have a Form 1099 to turn into the IRS when you file, you will be hit with a nasty surprise from the IRS that you owe them money and must file an amended tax return.

Here's another ugly surprise. The collection company can sell the unsettled portion of your debt to still another debt collector. The new collector can and will come after you. You may think that they cannot possibly legally do this, but they can. When the original creditor, say Discover Card, decided that you were not going to pay, they "charged off" your account. They then sold your account to a professional collector, sometimes for pennies on the dollar, depending on the age of the debt. That means the collection agency owns your debt, they can sell it, perfectly legal. So here just when you think you can finally relax with that monkey off your back you start getting collection calls again on the same debt from yet another collector harassing you for the unpaid portion. You have absolutely no protection, this as opposed to the protection you get from the legal system and the courts in bankruptcy. After you have been raked over the coals by some of these characters, bankruptcy starts looking pretty good.

Heed this cautionary tale from someone who has talked to many debt collectors. Just don't answer the phone, very simple. For some odd reason, people just have to answer the phone, like it would be impolite or politically incorrect not to. Where is it written that we have to answer the phone, especially for a debt collector? We live in a technological society where we actually get to see the number that is calling. If you do not know the number coming up on the screen, don't answer. If it is an 800 number, unavailable or restricted, chances are good it is a debt collector, many times from a foreign country.

When I read of advice to people being harassed by bill collectors, they will advise you to hang up on the collector. My question is, why would you answer in the first place, do you really want to talk to them? They are not your friend my friend.

If you must talk, do it on your own terms. And please, have a plan before you talk to them and do not deviate from it. If you talk to them without being in control of the situation, next thing you know you will be pledging your firstborn to them. Yes, they are that good. They want you to think you have no control or choice, but in fact you are the one who should be calling the shots, not them. Just try laying the word "bankruptcy" on them, oh no, they don't want you to do that. They will be quick to tell you what a mistake that would be and how it will ruin your life, like they are not already trying to do that. See what power you have and you don't even know it?

Take it from someone who has probably talked to more than fifty different debt collectors, they can be very persuasive. Collectors who are really good at their job make a lot of money, the more they collect, the more money they make. They will have you raiding your kid's piggy bank to get a check to them before you know what hit you. They can have you rattling off your bank account information like someone hypnotized. The power of a strange voice on the phone when you are in a vulnerable state is uncanny. They will feed on your fear. Giving a debt collector electronic assess to your bank accounts is even worse than giving your social security number to anyone that asks for it. Would you do that? The collectors expect, no they demand, that you give them electronic access to your accounts or they will not "help" you.

There is a particularly virulent debt collector out there called the "junk" debt collector, junk because it is valued so low by the creditor, so low that they will sell the debt for pennies on the dollar. Lest you be lulled into a false sense of security because those pesky debt collectors no longer hound you day and night, know that you could be in for a surprise. You may think (wishful thinking) that they have forgotten all about little old you and are off to bedevil some other poor soul. These companies that buy your old debt have a possible goldmine, whatever they can squeeze out of you will be mostly pure profit. This type of collector is probably the worst of the worst because they have already paid for the contract you had with the original creditor for the merest fraction of what you owed. Safe to say they have a powerful incentive to get you to pay up, or hound you to death in the process, whichever comes first.

Bad debts are forever lurking out there, ready to jump out and bite you just when you thought they have forgotten you. Maybe the original creditor won't but that hot shot debt collector that just bought your old debt will be more than happy to. Collecting ancient debt has become a very hot and prosperous business. Collectors can make fortunes squeezing these old debts out of the consumer. These are the most ruthless of the ruthless because they have so much to gain. If you had an unpaid debt of $5000 and the ancient junk collector paid ten cents on the dollar, they would have paid $500 for the contract you signed when you got the credit card that you now still owe $5000 on. That translates into a profit of $4500 for the debt collector. Often this collector is a few steps away from the original creditor. Remember, even if you settled a debt previously, that collector may have sold the unpaid portion, the amount you settled for subtracted from your balance owed. Previous arrangements and monies you paid on this account mean nothing to the new debt collector. To them, you are just someone who owes a debt and their one and only objective is to retrieve it.

Modern technology greatly benefits debt collectors. The internet is a treasure trove for finding people. They have access to your credit report, remember you granted that right to the original creditor, now every collector down the food chain has access to it. Probably a host of other sharks too. They can compile pertinent information which they can use to pursue you. It is relatively easy to find out how much equity you have in real estate. They know your mortgage balance from your credit report. It is ridiculously easy to find out the value of your property, no matter where on earth your property is thanks to all the sites on the internet that track property values. If they think you have any equity or other assets, you will be in their crosshairs.

The Fair Debt Collection Practices Act of 1977 was instituted to protect the debtor from unfair and harassing collection tactics. The Act spelled out what debt collectors could and could not do and when they could and could not do it.

The FDCPA addresses when debt collectors can contact you.
Section 805(a)

Without the prior consent of the consumer given directly to the debt collector or the express permission of a court of competent jurisdiction, a debt collector may not communicate with a consumer in connection with the collection of any debt

1. At any unusual time or place or at a time or place known or which should be known to be inconvenient to the consumer. In the absence of knowledge of circumstances to the contrary, a debt collector shall assume that the convenient time for communicating with a consumer is after 8:00 a.m. and before 9:00 p.m., local time at the consumer's location.

2. If the debt collector knows the consumer is represented by an attorney with respect to such debt and has knowledge of, or can readily ascertain, such attorney's name and address, unless the attorney fails to respond within a reasonable period of time to a communication from the debt

collector or unless the attorney consents to direct communication with the consumer.

Section 805(c)

If the consumer notifies a debt collector in writing that the consumer refuses to pay a debt or that the consumer wishes the debt collector to cease further communication with the consumer, the debt collector shall not communicate further with the consumer with respect to such debt, except-

1. To advise the consumer that the debt collector's further efforts are terminated;

2. To notify the consumer that the debt collector or creditor may invoke specified remedies which are ordinarily invoked by such debt collector or creditor; or

3. Where applicable, to notify the consumer that the debt collector or creditor intends to invoke a specified remedy. If such notice from the consumer is made by mail, notification shall be complete upon receipt.

Section 805(d)

For the purpose of this section, the term "consumer" includes the consumer's spouse, parent (if the consumer is a minor), guardian, executor or administrator.

The FDCPA addresses where debt collectors can contact you.

Section 805(a)

Without the prior consent of the consumer given directly to the debt collector or the express permission of a court of competent jurisdiction, a debt collector may not communicate with a consumer in connection with the collection of any debt at the consumer's place of employment if the debt collector knows or has reason to know that the consumer's employer prohibits the consumer from receiving such communication.

The FDCPA prohibits intimidation and harassment

Section 806

A debt collector may not engage in any conduct the natural consequence of which is to harass, oppress, or abuse any person in connection with the collection of a debt. Without limiting the general application of the foregoing, the following conduct is a violation of this section:

1. The use or threat of use of violence or other criminal means to harm the physical person, reputation, or property of any person.

2. The use of obscene or profane language or language the natural consequence of which is to abuse the hearer or reader.
3. The publication of a list of consumers who allegedly refuse to pay debts, except to a consumer reporting agency or to {persons having a legitimate interest in this information}
4. The advertisement for sale of any debt to coerce payment of the debt.
5. Causing a telephone to ring or engaging any person in telephone conversation repeatedly or continuously with intent to annoy, abuse, or harass any person at the called number.
6. Except as provided in section 804, the placement of telephone calls without meaningful disclosure of the caller's identity.

The FDCPA prohibits dirty tricks and tactics

Section 807

A debt collector may not use any false, deceptive, or misleading representations or means in connection with the collection of any debt. Without limiting the general application of the foregoing, the following is a violation of this section:

1. The false representation or implication that the debt collector is vouched for, bonded by, or affiliated with the United States or any State, including the use of any badge, uniform, or facsimile thereof.
2. The false representation of-
   A. the character, amount, or legal status of any debt; or
   B. any services rendered or compensation which may be lawfully received by any debt collector for the collection of a debt.
3. The false representation or implication that any individual is an attorney or that any communication is from an attorney.
4. The representation or implication that nonpayment of any debt will result in the arrest or imprisonment of any person or the seizure, garnishment, attachment, or sale of any property or wages of any person unless such action is lawful and the debt collector or creditor intends to take such action.
5. The threat to take any action that cannot legally be taken or that is not intended to be taken.

6. The false representation or implication that a sale, referral, or other transfer of any interest in a debt shall cause the consumer to-

   A. lose any claim or defense to payment of the debt; or

   B. become subject to any practice prohibited by this {act}

7. The false representation or implication that the consumer committed any crime or other conduct in order to disgrace the consumer.

8. Communicating or threatening to communicate to any person credit information which is known or which should be known to be false, including the failure to communicate that a disputed debt is disputed.

9. The use or distribution of any written communication which simulates or is falsely represented to be a document authorized, issued, or approved by any court, official, or agency of the United States or any State, or which creates a false impression as to its source, authorization, or approval.

10. The use of any false representation or deceptive means to collect or attempt to collect any debt or to obtain information concerning a consumer.

11. Except as otherwise provided for {under section 804, which allows inquiries to determine a debtor's whereabouts; section 804 is discussed in more detail later in this appendix} the failure to disclose clearly in all communications made to collect a debt or to obtain information about a consumer, that the debt collector is attempting to collect a debt and that any information obtained will be used for that purpose.

12. The false representation or implication that accounts have been turned over to innocent purchasers for value.

13. The false representation or implication that documents are legal process.

14. The use of any business, company, or organization name other than the true name of the debt collector's business, company, or organization.

15. The false representation or implication that documents are not legal process forms or do not require action by the consumer.

16. The false representation or implication that a debt collector operates or is employed by a consumer reporting agency as defined {in the Fair Credit Reporting Act}

Section 808

A debt collector may not use unfair or unconscionable means to collect or attempt to collect any debt. Without limiting the general application of the foregoing, the following conduct is a violation of this section:

1. The collection of any amount (including any interest, fee, charge, or expense incidental to the principal obligation) unless such amount is expressly authorized by the agreement creating the debt or permitted by law.

2. The acceptance by a debt collector from any person of a check or other payment instrument postdated by more than five days unless such person is notified in writing of the debt collector's intent to deposit such check or instrument not more than ten nor less than three business days prior to such deposit.

3. The solicitation by a debt collector of any postdated check or other postdated payment instrument prior to the date on such check or instrument.

4. Depositing or threatening to deposit any postdated check or other postdated payment instrument prior to the date on such check or instrument.

5. Causing charges to be made to any person for communication by conceal-ment of the true purpose of the communication. Such charges include, but are not limited to, collect telephone calls and telegram fees.

6. Taking or threatening to take any judicial action to effect dispossession or disablement of property if-

   A. there is no present right to possession of the property claim as collateral through an enforceable security interest; or

   B. there is no present intention to take possession or disablement; or

   C. the property is exempt by law from such dispossession or disablement.

7. Communicating with a consumer regarding a debt by post card.

8. Using any language or symbol, other than the debt collector's address, on any envelope when communicating with a consumer by use of the mails or by telegram, except that a debt collector may use his business name if such name does not indicate that he is in the debt collection business.

The FDCPA regulates when debt collectors may contact others about your debt.

Section 804

Any debt collector communicating with any person other than the consumer for the purpose of acquiring location information about a consumer shall-

1. Identify himself, state that he is confirming or correcting location information concerning the consumer, and, only if expressly requested, identify his employer:

2. Not state that such consumer owes any debt:

3. Not communicate with any such person more than once unless requested to do so by such person or unless the debt collector reasonably believes that the earlier response of such person is erroneous or incomplete and that such person now has correct or complete location information:

4. Not communicate by post card:

5. Not use any language or symbol on any envelope or in the contents of any communication effected by the mails or telegram that indicates that the debt collector is in the debt collection business or that the communication relates to the collection of a debt; and

6. After the debt collector knows the consumer is represented by an attorney with regard to the subject debt and has knowledge of, or can readily ascertain, such attorney's name and address, not communicate with any person other than that attorney, unless the attorney fails to respond within a reasonable period of time to communication from the debt collector.

Section 805(b)

Except as provided in Section 804, without the prior consent of the consumer given directly to the debt collector, or the express permission of a court of competent jurisdiction, or as reasonably necessary to effectuate a post judgment judicial remedy, a debt collector may not communicate, in connection with the collection of any debt, with any person other than the consumer, his attorney, a consumer reporting agency if otherwise permitted by law the creditor, the attorney of the creditor, or the attorney for the debt collector.

You may be thinking to yourself that you have talked to many debt collectors who apparently didn't get the Fair Debt Collection Practice Act memo.

So what are your recourses? The FDCPA grants you the right to sue the debt collector and collect up to $1,000 in damages.

Section 813(a)

Except as otherwise provided by this section, any debt collector who fails to comply with any provision of this title with respect to any person is liable to such person in an amount equal to the sum of-

1. Any actual damages sustained by such person as a result of such failure;
2. In the case of any action by an individual, such additional damages as the court may allow, but not exceeding $1,000;
3. In the case of any successful action to enforce the foregoing liability, the costs of the action, together with a reasonable attorney's fee as determined by the court. On a finding by the court that an action under this section was brought in bad faith and for the purpose of harassment, the court may award to the defendant attorney's fees reasonable in relation to the work expended and costs.

Section 813(d)

An action to enforce any liability created by this title may be brought in any appropriate United States district court without regard to the amount in controversy, or in any other court of competent jurisdiction, within one year from the date on which the violation occurs.

CHAPTER EIGHT

DEBT MANAGEMENT, DEBT SETTLEMENT, DEBT CONSOLIDATION AND JUDGMENTS

Credit card debt has spawned a cottage industry that has sprung up to "help" the consumer with the debt problems. These players are the debt management, debt settlement and debt consolidation companies. The problem is it is usually the players getting helped, not you, your problems are only getting worse.

The debt management company will be only too happy to help your nasty old debt problem go away simply and painlessly. Of course it will most likely leave you worse off than you were in the first place. You saw an ad on television. A debt management company can cut your monthly payments in half, but do they tell you it will take twice as long, if not more? This is called re-aging, it means that they will tack it on at the end. For example let's say you missed three payments of $100. Instead of making you pay the $300, they will "allow" you to pay only $150. But you did not gain a thing, that extra $150 is just added to the back end of the loan, you are still going to pay it. The debt management company will tell you that bankruptcy is bad for you, that it is a lifetime mistake. They have an agenda, they can make a lot of money off you but if you file for bankruptcy there goes their cash cow. Your biggest mistake will be in believing them!

Far too often debtors who participate in debt management spend thousands of dollars that they could have instead kept by filing for bankruptcy protection. If you are depleting your exempt property by refinancing and equity lines of credit to make your debt management payments, you are taking a giant risk and you stand a very good chance of losing your home. The irony of this is that you could file for bankruptcy protection and still keep the property. Losing your family's home has to be one of life's most crushing and debilitating blows, far worse than any bankruptcy could ever be.

When you are in a debt management program, you are paying for debts that are dischargeable in a bankruptcy. Many fear filing for bankruptcy because they think they cannot obtain credit. If you are that over-extended, you would not be able to get credit anyway. You may ask yourself why getting credit again is one of your concerns. Look where credit has gotten you. The truth is however that you will be able to get credit much sooner with a bankruptcy. Think of it this way, a bankruptcy will not look much worse on your credit report than carrying delinquent debt, regardless of what the economic pundits say. Credit card companies know you cannot file again for a period of two to three years, they got you on the hook, again. The ink was not dry on our bankruptcy filing when the offers from creditors started coming.

While the premise of working with a debt management company is enticing, who doesn't want someone else to just take this burden off their hands, know that the benefit you think you are getting could come with a very high price. The job of the debt manager is to work with the debtor on helping them pay back their creditors. They will call the collection agencies and credit card companies and negotiate on your behalf, they will be your agent. They, supposedly, will get your interest rate lowered, have removed various charges to your account, and act as a go-between you and the creditor. For this service they are paid out of your payments, and paid handsomely. Talk about relinquishing control. You have just given a total stranger, a disembodied voice on the phone, access to your money. And they didn't even use a gun. Yes, I understand that you will be more than happy to pay someone to take this mess off your hands, but you may find the price very high, financially and emotionally.

How do you know they are applying payments to your account in a timely manner, or maybe not at all? Maybe they have absconded with money and are now setting up business in another state. There are probably good and reputable companies providing debt management services but there are many, many who are scam artists and will only drive you further down the hole you find yourself in. How do you know which kind you are handing over your money to?

The debt management companies will be quick to assure you are making the right choice engaging them to handle your debt and that they will save you from bankruptcy, but who is saving you from them? Let's assume for a minute that the debt management is legitimate and will actually do what they promise to do. Remember these companies are making money from the money you are paying them to send to the creditor. They are charging you a fee, a hefty fee, to do this job for you. Know this, you can negotiate just as well yourself. Don't hand your finances over to a perfect stranger. This is precisely what you do when you engage a debt management company. The best case scenario is that they pay your creditors as promised, and charge you a lot of money to do so. Worst case scenario, they take your money and run. Neither of the possibilities sound like the best solution to your debt problems.

Remember this, debt management companies are really just debt collectors in disguise. Often the debt management companies are working for the creditor. The creditor is trying to get their money one way or another. The credit card companies embrace the debt management companies because they help them recoup at least some or all of the debt owed. A debt management company will require you to pay your debt in full in addition to any finance charges and fees. While you are in debt management, you still have no protection from creditors, they can still, and do, sue you. When you are under the bankruptcy protection "umbrella" you are protected from your creditors. I don't know about you but I would rather have the law on my side.

Often in debt management programs, the debtor's budget is cut to the bone and they are constantly short of cash every month and they must struggle every month to get by. It is common that when someone realizes they are getting nowhere with the management plan and decide to save themselves by filing bankruptcy, they find their monthly expenses drop by hundreds of dollars. That means you have extra money each month, hundreds of dollars as a matter of fact. Extra money, what a concept. Many people who finally choose bankruptcy say that they only wished they had done it sooner and saved themselves a lot of money and pain

Debt management programs may work for people with manageable debt and who do not have to live at a subsistence level to keep up with the plan. If this doesn't sound like you, you may want to rethink that oh-so enticing offer of the debt management company to "rescue" you.

Debt consolidation companies are another player in the lucrative field of debt riddled consumers. This is the ultimate shell game. You cannot get out of debt just by re-arranging it. Nor can you borrow your way out of debt, that surely must be an oxymoron. Yes, I know, it sounds so darn good, put all your bills together and pay just one easy payment a month. However that one "easy" payment could go on forever and turn out to be not so easy.

With debt consolidation, you are in a debt repayment plan, just as you are with debt management. Sometimes debt consolidation and debt management companies do cross over, but know they are not the same. With debt consolidation, you take out one loan to pay off all the rest of your loans. You can, in some instances, get an unsecured "jumbo" loan to pay off your other unsecured debt, like credit card and medical debt. The interest rate paid for these loans is high. The majority of debt consolidation loans however are secured by pledging collateral, such as your house. You are trading your unsecured debt for secured debt, your precious home. You put your house as risk. It happens all the time, it almost happened to me. How ironic, you end up losing your home when you could have been protected by the bankruptcy laws from your creditors AND kept your home.

Know that when you consolidate your debts, you are going to stretch your payments out longer and stay in debt longer. Translation. Your path to recovery and prosperity is pushed further and further down the road, if ever. Yes your total payment might be smaller than all your previous payments put together, but the smaller the payment, the longer in years you will have to pay. Don't forget the hefty fees for this loan either. When you are paying for years and years on this seemingly never-ending plan, you have also lost those very same precious years that you could have been spending on rebounding to prosperity. They say time is money. That is not true. Time is far more important than money. You can always make money but you cannot make more time, time is finite, money is infinite.

Debt consolidation is not that easy to get. The very best terms are reserved for people with good credit. That probably is not you at this point. You will pay a very high interest rate for your loan. Translation, very little is going to the principal, translation, you will be paying for a long, long time. Know that the "counselors" working for these companies are great salesman. They are selling you on the idea that they will be your knight in shining armor, rescuing you from the financial mess you have made of your life. However, they will be the ones reaping a financial benefit, not you.

DEBT MANAGEMENT, DEBT SETTLEMENT, DEBT CONSOLIDATION AND JUDGMENTS

To many consumers debt consolidation is nothing but a placebo, they think they are doing something good for their financial life but really they are not. They are just trading one debt for another, probably worse. They are lulled into a false sense of security, thinking they are being proactive about their debt problem when truthfully they are inviting their debt to move in with them and, like a stubborn house guest, you cannot get them out.

Debt settlement companies are another player in the industry. Debt wracked people are especially vulnerable to this scheme. You see these lovely commercials on television. A man and woman are agonizing over their debt when they are told to just pick up the phone and call this number and all their debt problems will fly out the window.

Debt settlement is extremely expensive. Often you need to pay large up front fees for them to set up your "account". If you have no money to pay them now, they will "let" you roll the fees into your monthly payments, of course ballooning your monthly payment. The fee may be paid right off the top of the money you are depositing into your account. In other words, they are getting paid before any of your money is going to the creditor. In addition to the upfront fees that they are rolling, (inflating) into your monthly payment, you will also have to pay monthly fees throughout the duration of the program. In other words, fees are the new interest. You may feel like you went from the frying pan into the fire. All this and you still have no protection from your creditors. They can, and do, file lawsuits against you whether you are in a debt program or not.

Debt settlement companies are outlawed in Arizona, Georgia, Hawaii, Louisiana, Maine, Mississippi, New Jersey, New Mexico, New York, North Dakota, West Virginia and Wyoming. If you happen to live in one of those states and are working with a debt settlement company they are doing it illegally, even if they are located in a state that doesn't prohibit them.

Many may think that debt settlement is preferable to bankruptcy, that it does not carry the same stigma. Many debtors will chose debt settlement over bankruptcy as it is not as "bad" as bankruptcy, so they think.

The high cost of settlement breaks down like this. You agree to send them, or they will electronically take it out of your account, money every month. This will be an amount based not on what you can afford but what you owe. Add to that their fee. Typically the fee can run from ten to twenty percent. That percentage is based on what you owe, not what they can negotiate it down for. If you have total debt of $40,000, and their fee is fifteen percent, they will charge you $6000 to settle your debt, no matter what amount they can get it down to. That payment you send every month typically goes into an escrow account, being accumulated into a "lump" sum that the debt settlement company will offer to the creditor as a "settlement in full" of your debts. Of course they have access to your money in this account, you don't.

Settlement plans typically run for three years. But of course they could stretch it out longer, to make it more convenient for you. The longer you pay, the more money they make. Let's say that your plan is for three years. Assuming still you owe $40,000 in debt, they will set a monthly repayment plan for a "promised" 50% reduction in your debt. They will set up a plan for $20,000. Divide that by 36 months and the payment is $555. But don't forget the fee of 15%, that is another $166 a month for a total payment of $722. And no guarantee that they can deliver the reduced payment. The debt settlement offers you no guarantee. You pay your money faithfully and hope the debt settlement can pull your butt out of the fire. They may be able to settle with some but not everyone. It only takes one creditor to come after you to wipe out whatever advantage you gained with debt settlement. You are putting a lot of faith out there for very little chance of resolution to your crushing debt problem.

So you sign up for debt settlement. There, now you have taken care of the problem. The next time that pesky collector calls you can disdainfully tell them "you are working with a debt settlement counselor". Yeah, that will really impress them. They will continue to pursue you for the money whether you are with a debt settlement company or not. They can still bring a lawsuit and they will win. So there you are, in debt settlement and still being sued.

There may be some legitimate debt settlement companies out there but how do you know for sure that you are dealing with one of them. You are talking to someone on the phone or on line, giving them all your important information. You are to trust them to do what they promise you they will do. What is your recourse if they don't? Debt settlement is fraught with risks. It offers you no protection from lawsuits and liens. Your creditors will continue to hound you. Your phone won't stop ringing. What kind of resolution is that? The majority of debt settlement clients drop out after a few short months, file for bankruptcy and wish they had done that in the first place.

Debt settlement is a great unknown with no guarantee of how it will play out. You hope someday you will have this paid off, provided this was a legitimate company and was applying your payments as promised. There is always the very real possibility they will abscond with your money, many found that out the hard way. Once you have money invested in your "plan", you are afraid to stop because you fear losing the money you have already put in.

Debt settlement companies have people who are very good at their jobs. They will tell you that this must be your lucky day, you called them. When you tell them that you are considering bankruptcy they will fall all over themselves telling you that would be a 10 year mistake. They will assure you that attorneys would demand their fees up front, not like them of course. They will remind you how almost impossible it is to get a bankruptcy since the law was changed in 2005. They will then swoop in for their kill shot. "If I could solve your credit card debt would you be interested in our program?" How many desperate debtors could resist that line? It is probably the first line they learn in training.

Don't be fooled by the "not for profit" status some debt management, debt settlement and debt consolidation claim. We tend to think that if something is non-profit, they are making no money. And if they are making no money, how can they be making money off me. The fact is they are making a profit, a huge one, at your expense.

After we have the debt management, debt consolidation and debt settlement, we next have the dreaded judgments. You do not want a judgment against you. A judgment is the creditors most dreaded weapon. A creditor files a lawsuit against you because you owe them money. You become a defendant. It is Chase, Discover, Capitol One, plaintiff, against you, the defendant. You will receive a very official looking document from the court. You will be required to appear in court on a given day. Failure to do so could result in your arrest. So of course you go because you don't want the sheriff coming to your door to arrest you. As you owe the money, you have no defense. The creditor is awarded a judgment against you. Now they are armed with a powerful tool to use against you. They can garnish your wages, wipe out every penny you have in accounts and place liens against your property. The judgment will be entered into your credit report, and there it will sit, probably forever, surely at least until you pay it back.

When you have a judgment, you are required, by law, to pay. This is not some pesky debt collector harassing you, this is the court system and you don't want to mess around with the court system. There is no question that the creditor will obtain a judgment, they will obtain a judgment. There is no defense. You cannot go to court and tell the judge you lost your job, your child was sick, you got a divorce, laid off or fired. You can not escape the fact that you owe the money. The judge will award the creditor a judgment against you and if you thought your life was hell before dealing with debt collectors, you are up against the big guns now.

You will be required to fill out paperwork declaring all your assets and income. If you omit anything, that is perjury and that is a crime. If in anticipation of a judgment coming you transferred property in order to hide it from a creditor, that could also be an illegal transfer of property for the purpose of hindering or defrauding a creditor. The law calls it a fraudulent conveyance. That is also true if you transfer property out of your name before filing for bankruptcy.

Fear of a judgment is the reason you never want to ignore any correspondence from the court. Mail will usually come certified so you must sign for it although I have gotten correspondence from the court just through first class mail. Never ignore any correspondence from the court. A judgment can be entered against you without you ever showing up in court, you find out when you go to your bank and your accounts are wiped out. Yes, they can do that. They can take your money, cars, boats, and jewelry. I heard of a lady who was made to take off her wedding rings by the judge and turn them over to the court when a judgment was won against her. They could make you empty your pockets and purse and if you have anything of value, they can take it, then and there. They can ask you for your car title and you have to surrender it. This is legal and it happens all too often.

Once a creditor has won a judgment against you, they are allowed by law to collect interest on the amount you owe until it is paid, if ever. Your debt will grow instead of shrink. You can also be forced to pay the creditors legal fees.

Garnishments cannot be taken from your paycheck unless there is a judgment. A garnishment is not going to be some surprise one payday when you receive your check. You will know it is coming, unless of course you threw away that letter from the court.

When the creditor is awarded the judgment against you, they get what is called a "writ of garnishment". This will go to your employer and your bank to garnish your wages or empty your account, or at least of the amount that you owe the creditor. You will not be given a heads up. You will be notified only after your employment and bank have been notified. By that time it is too late to remove your money from the bank and hide it under your mattress. You may wonder how much they can take from your paycheck. They will look at the amount of your check after all your deductions required by law have been taken out. That does not include any savings, pension plan contributions or health insurance payments. It does include federal and state income tax and social se-curity. What is left is your disposable income, more commonly known as "take home pay". You know, the amount we actually get to keep.

If your take home pay is under $170 a week, you just got lucky, your wages cannot be garnished. If your take home pay is over $170 a week, they can take 25% right off the top, before you even see your check. Ouch! Having your wages garnished by a judgment is not legal grounds for an employer to fire you. But if they want to, they will. The burden would be on you to prove it.

If a creditor has a judgment and garnished your bank account and you do not know it yet, any check you wrote on the money that they took from your account will bounce. You will be responsible for any fees for returned checks. You cannot complain to the bank that you didn't know they were going to that therefore it is not your fault that your checks bounced.

The very worst case scenario with a judgment is that the court can force you to sell your home to pay the debts. The exception is if the judgment is for $3000 or less. Any judgment over $3000, you can lose your home. That would be crazy. You should never let your situation come to that. Why would you let yourself lose secured property due to unsecured debt? Remember if you default on your debt, the creditor is out for blood. They want everything you have, all of which are worth far, far more than probably all the stuff you put on plastic combined. Yes I know that often we ran up that debt just trying to survive, buying groceries, medicines, utilities and even the mortgage. By the same token, many people simply ran up huge amounts of debts because, well because they could. Whatever the reason, and probably for most it is a mixture of reasons, a bankruptcy grants us a second chance to wipe the slate clean.

Judgments are bad, you don't want one, or fifteen in my case if I had let it get that far. They are really worse than bankruptcy because they don't go away. They will languish around the rest of your life to wreck havoc on you. With bankruptcy, you know there is an expiration date, when it is discharged, it is over. With a judgment, there is no expiration date. They are good for ten years but they can always be extended, probably into infinity, or at least until you die.

Debt management companies, debt settlement companies and debt consolidation companies are not the welcome answer to your debt problems. Bankruptcy affords you the very best opportunity of having a future. You do have one you know, even though at times when you're going through severe financial crisis you would swear you have no future. I know the feeling.

One reason that is often given for reluctance to file bankruptcy is the rather bizarre notion that it will hurt your credit score. Eh, excuse me, I would bet your credit is pretty bad right now if you have high debt, late or missed payments and collectors calling you. How much worse do you think a bankruptcy will be to the almighty Holy Grail, your FICA score? With a bankruptcy this whole mess is neatly and legally tied up in a neat package and you are on your way up, not down. Yes a bankruptcy, odd as it may sound, means you are finally going in the right direction.

It is far better to have a bankruptcy than to have liens and judgments against you, your property and your credit report. For those of you who fear they will never be able to buy a home because of a bankruptcy, you will certainly be able to. As of now the underwriting for a mortgage makes you wait two years after the discharge of a bankruptcy to be able to get a loan for a home.

Bankruptcy legally wipes out debt, you can consider yourself cleansed by the courts. When you have liens and judgments, you must pay them off before getting a mortgage. Bankruptcy is sanctioned by the law, how much better can it get? Many fear bankruptcy as they hate being involved in the "legal" system. But like it or not, when you are hit with lawsuits and liens, you are involved with the court system and they are not on your side.

CHAPTER NINE

WHY PLASTIC IS HAZARDOUS TO YOUR WEALTH

We have heard it said the borrower is slave to the lender. Credit card debt will plunge you into servitude before you even know it. Plastic is not real, it is an illusion. It will lull you into debt, every so delicately, or not. Plastic debt is the number one cause of bankruptcy.

We get plastic because we want to, we use plastic because we have to. We have to so much eventually we get to our limit. Then we cannot use it anymore and we have no money because we are sending a disproportionate amount of our money to the creditors. Now we have no money and no credit. That is a scary place to be. You just know in your heart that an emergency is just around the corner and you will need money/credit and you cannot get either.

When we use plastic, we are charging our future for our past. That dinner you charged last night will be in a waste treatment plant within a day and your money with it. Talk about return. At least if you paid for your meal with cash (or debit, same thing) the price you paid is already in the past, not the future. With plastic, the price is always in the future. You are in effect mortgaging your future. For what?

What is the power and mystique of pulling out plastic and buying something with money you don't have? You are making the purchase based on the assumption that you will have the money to pay for it next month. But what happens more often than not is that next month can grow to infinity. You can be paying for a purchase 10 years after you made it, long after it has probably ended up in the garbage or in a garage sale, fetching maybe 1/20th of what you paid for it.

People love plastic because it gives a sense of power. We can get whatever we want whenever we want, provided we are not already at our limit, without having a dollar in our wallet or money in a debit account. We also get those real cool gifts when we apply for credit. I have a stadium blanket that only cost $3000.

Did you ever consider that when you use a credit card and are not among the minority of customers that pay off their bill in full every month, you are taking out a loan where you do not know what the total cost will be nor how long you will be paying on it? Imagine this. You go to the bank to get a loan to buy a house or a car. You ask the lender how much your interest rate would be, what your payments will be and how long it will take to pay off the loan. If they told you they didn't know would you still take out the loan? Would you take on that obligation and liability without knowing what it would cost? That is exactly what you do when you use plastic.

You have no idea how much that $25 meal at McDonalds or the $1500 plasma TV is really costing. Once the interest, late fees, jacked-up interest, double billing and whatever fees and penalties they can sock you with are worked into the balance you would have to have the mind of a computer chip to actually figure out the exact cost of anything you put on plastic.

Another negative in using plastic is that it doesn't hurt so bad. Swiping a card is far easier than handing over cash. We can disassociate our self from actually "paying" by using plastic. It isolates the pain from parting with our money, it's only a piece of plastic. This detachment feeds overspending, you buy more stuff, pay more for the stuff and are less aware of how much money you have actually spent on stuff.

When you pay with plastic, your purchases are pretty much lumped together, not on your statement of course but in your mind. This is but another form of disassociation we employ. It is oh so easy to get carried away with plastic when our purchases get lost in a sea of charges on your statement. That $50 you charged for dinner loses its effectiveness to sting when it is surround by a host of other charges. Spending $2000 for a Mexican vacation when were already deeply in debt is a perfect example.

It is a well accepted fact that consumers have a love affair with plastic because they see it as "convenient". Let's just agree that we all love convenience. But for that convenience, you will pay a very high price. Once you open up that particular Pandora's Box of plastic, you are engaged in a toxic relationship, one that will poison the well of your being and your quality of life, often for a very, very long time, maybe forever. I too loved credit cards for convenience. Long before using credit cards to float the construction project, I was using plastic for, well just about everything. The truth is that debt encourages poverty, not prosperity.

The consumer is no match for a credit card company's bag of tricks. Realize that the deck is stacked against you. You can't outfox them. The credit card companies have powerful lobbyists on their side, lobbying machines that spent $83 million in 2008 alone. These figures show the immense power of the banking industry. We, the consumers, don't stand a chance against them.

Credit card companies and banking are light years ahead of us. Even the "good" paying customers are not spared. The credit card companies really don't like it when people pay their bill in full every month, how are they to make any money if they can't gouge the customer with interest? A favorite trick is to shrink the grace period window which in turn ups the odds that even the most conscientious of customers will sooner or later be late with a payment. That one little oversight can double or triple their interest rate. The only difference between the credit card company squeezing you and a loan shark is the credit card company most likely won't break your kneecaps.

Credit card companies are like those lasers that museums have to keep a thief from stealing its' treasures, you have to know exactly where those laser beams are to avoid them. It is very easy to step over invisible boundaries. Yes I know credit card companies will decry, "it's in the fine print" and it probably is, buried in language an attorney would have trouble deciphering. Credit card companies routinely raise your interest rate if your credit score falls. What logic follows that raising a customer's interest rate because they are carrying a lot of debt is a good thing. They have just increased the chances of the customer defaulting. You wonder what brainiacs are in charge. Sounds like the patients are running the asylum.

It is easy to put a number to debt. In the United States alone, the collective debt is 972.5 billion. Whenever they talk about the average household debt, the number is around $12,000 owed in credit card debt. There were many times I wished I lived in that household with only $12,000 worth of debt. But what about the human side of debt, that is a lot harder to ascertain. One in every 5 households in America are living in credit card crisis. Either they are behind in their payments or are at the credit limit, often times both.

When we have debt in our life, it is never an isolated issue. It spills over into every aspect of our life. It affects our marriage, our children, our jobs and our mental health. Who has not lain awake at night, juggling in their mind how they are possibly going to pull it off yet another month. How many of us engage in the credit card shuffle just to make it one more month.

This crushing worry over debt has driven otherwise rational human beings right over the edge. One woman killed herself because she and her husband were so deeply in debt. She left a note for her husband to take her insurance money to pay off their debts. She must not have known that insurance policies do not pay off on suicide. That is probably a good thing because many more people might try that route if the insurance did pay off. A man who was deeply in credit card debt and also facing foreclosure robbed a bank. Now he will spend many years in prison, exacerbating the situation grievously for his family.

Desperate people do desperate things. Desperation almost made me take out a toxic loan on our house to try and pay off the credit card debt. If I had done that we surely would have lost it to foreclosure. But many people crippled with debt are not as lucky, they make bad decisions because they are so desperate and vulnerable. Credit card debt is so debilitating and insidious, it should come with a warning label, like cigarettes.

When we are so wracked with worry about our debt, it can't help but have an adverse effect on our performance at work. At the time you need the money the very most you are jeopardizing your employment with worry and preoccupation. It is so very hard to concentrate on a job when you are constantly obsessing and worrying about your debt that mysteriously seems to grow bigger every month despite your scrimping to send the minimum each month. Worry about debt is the number one reason for stress. But hey you did not need me to tell you that.

As if you were not paying a high price already worrying yourself to death over your debt, you need to put up with the debt collectors calling you. I love it when they tell you that you missed a payment, or three, like you don't know that already. That statement is followed up with a request to give them your bank information so that they may electronically extract the payment today, for your convenience of course. If the worry over the debt isn't killing you, the debt collectors will surely finish you off.

Couples fight over money, sex and children. You notice money comes before even sex. Debt has caused many a marriage to end in divorce. What a tragedy, talk about collateral damage. The burden of debt not only affects you and your spouse, it affects your children and their future. Children are very perceptive, they know there is trouble and that impacts their lives adversely. Besides the emotional dynamics of a financial disaster looming in their life, they also face a bleaker prospect in their own future. It is much harder to educate our children when we are drowning in debt. Sure they could probably get loans to pay for their college education and many do and it works out. However they are starting out already with huge student loans to repay, not a real auspicious start in life. It may be hard to ever play catch up. They will have to run even faster to keep up, often never being able to get out from behind the eight ball. What an unfortunate legacy to hand down.

We know that children learn by what they see and hear. If they see their parents getting in way over their heads due to credit card debt, they will think that is probably normal, even though they may hear their parents fighting about it. It is a proven fact that children mimic their parents. Getting into credit card debt is not something we should be passing onto our children. Even though they can see how detrimental debt can be, that does not mean they will be repelled by it. We know that children who were abused will often abuse their own children. The same is true if the parent was an alcoholic, a gambler or drug abuser.

Somehow we have evolved into a species that believe we got to have it all. No, we don't want to save for it, we want it now. Having it now often means paying with plastic, because while we want it now, we don't have the money now. So we put it on plastic and pay for it later. The problem with that is that later comes much sooner than you think and it comes with a hefty price tag. That item that you had to have now can very easily end up costing you twice as much, if not more. Not only are we mortgaging our future, and our family's, we are reinforcing that immediate gratification disease that we are afflicted with. More often than not, delayed gratification is so much more satisfying, and so much cheaper. If you think about it, we can actually end up with more by practicing a little delayed gratification. If we are not so busy throwing our money away with both hands at the credit card companies today, we will have far more purchasing power tomorrow.

"Buy now, pay later". How many times have we heard this. When we buy on plastic today we are lining up for the dubious distinction of getting to pay far more for merchandise than the amount it is priced at. When we buy a computer for $1000 at an interest rate of 18% and pay only the minimum, that computer will end up costing you almost twice as much, $1800. What could you have done with that extra $800? We need to learn to save for things we want, just think of how much more we could have if we did that instead of using plastic. The only ones prospering from plastic are the credit card companies, not you and I. They are prospering at our expense, we have to be smarter than that. Don't make the credit card companies prosperous, let's make ourselves prosperous.

On the subject of paying only the minimum, which is what so many of us do, we can be paying for the rest of our lives. When we pay the minimum, we are hardly making a dent in the principle. The higher your interest rate is, the less of your payment goes to the principal every month. Throw in some late charges, over limit charges and any other "gotcha" charges and you will find your balance growing every month, in spite of dipping into the grocery money just to make the payment.

"One year, same as cash". If the full amount is not paid off in that year, the interest will then be calculated retroactive back to the date of the purchase. The couch you bought for $800 same as cash for one year suddenly is going to cost you twice as much, or more. All perfectly legal. While consumers have the best intentions of paying it off in a year, often times it does not work out that way.

Even if you are a customer who has excellent credit and are offered a card for very low or even 0 interest, beware. It may even say it is for the life of the card. Then you really need to beware. Why would one of the greediest big businesses on the planet offer something for nothing? Even if you pay faithfully every month, you may inadvertently trigger the universal default policy. You will then see your 0 interest jump to 29%. If they check your credit report, and they can anytime they want, and find out you're carrying a lot of debt or are too close to your credit line, they can raise your rate. It happened to me and it can happen to you.

If you need any more proof that credit card companies are sneaky at best and practically criminal at worst, they have another favorite ploy to further fleece and mislead the consumer called bait and switch. A credit card company will offer a wonderful primo rate to the card holder, maybe even a 0 rate. They then add onto your new account an old charged off debt from a past creditor. Can they do this? You bet, they bought your debt from a lender you defaulted on. They could have also bought it from a lender who took a settlement in lieu of the whole amount you paid them. It is no different from collectors selling the un-paid portion of your settled debt to another collector.

When you live your life with plastic in it, you are vulnerable to a host of possible scenarios, none of them good. It seems that the very slightest misstep can condemn you to a whole series of nasty things coming your way. Once we are in so far, it is almost like the point of no return. When the hemorrhaging starts and you find yourself in a freefall without a net, you wonder how and when it will all end.

The United States Federal Reserve cut its rate to 1%. Do you think maybe the credit card customer could get a little break from high credit card interest? Not a chance. In fact credit card companies are raising rates. Why? They are faced with huge losses from charge-offs, debts they have determined to be uncollectible, a situation largely brought on themselves by sucking the customer dry. Why couldn't the credit card companies be satisfied with a reasonable rate of return? That might have made all the difference between the debtor being able to pay as promised rather than being driven into the ground under the impossible burden laid on them by the creditor. Just asking. Ironic too, they will benefit from the tax write off they derive from the charge off. Add that to what they sold your debt for. They do know how to narrow their losses.

Creditors have always been punitive to consumers with less than perfect credit and now they are even going after their "A" customers. No matter that your credit score is good, you will still pay more for credit. The credit card companies certainly will not suck up the loss, it will be passed onto the consumer, you. That is unless we outwit them and not use plastic anymore.

Be assured that your credit card company can, and will, raise your interest rate whenever they want to. According to CNN, Citi Group got a bailout of 20 billion. They then turned around and raised their customers interest rate 2 to 3 percent. They also leveled a charge of 11% for ATM withdrawals. They then laid off 50,000 workers and used some of the bail out money to purchase other distressed banks. Citi Group got the bailout and customers got the shaft. Business as usual.

We use plastic because we don't have the money now. Next month when we get our statement owing considerably more than we charged, we can't buy the goods we need this month because we have to pay off last month's purchases. And so the cycle continues, grinding you further and further down the abyss. What is happening is your debts are snowballing, gathering more indebtedness until there is no way you can ever get out. Your $10,000 debt mushrooms to $20,000. What you're putting on plastic today will cost twice as much or more before this whole sordid mess is played out. How long can you afford to keep up?

Know that if you default on your credit card debt, legally the creditor can take all you hold dear, all that is so much more important than all you bought on credit put together. Your purchases on plastic will never offer you a return, it is not an investment, they probably depreciated the minute you acquired them. Money and missed opportunities, lost forever.

Plastic is insidious. It is like cancer, its metastasized tentacles reaching every part of your life. It is time to stop the madness.

CHAPTER TEN

WHY BANKRUPTCY?

Why you ask? Why not? The alternatives ain't pretty. It makes far more sense to stop briefly and take your "time out" with a bankruptcy as opposed to struggling for years and years to pay off unmanageable debt and suffering through collections and lawsuits.

With a bankruptcy you are given the opportunity to get on with your life. When you are stuck in debt that you cannot conceivably pay off your life is on hold and as for your future, you may ask yourself "what future".

Often when we are in a financial crisis the first response is to cut back on contributing to our retirement plan. That is a terrible and destructive move, not to mention counterproductive. Talk about jeopardizing the future! Your retirement will be protected in a bankruptcy, why would you even consider sacrificing that?

A bankruptcy is not an evil, it is a tool for survival. Does the prospect of having your life back appeal to you? You will not only get your life back, you will get your future back.

I had surgery a few years back. When I woke up in the recovery room I was freezing. Anyone who has had surgery knows they keep the surgical rooms cold. While laying there is my cold misery someone put a hot blanket on top of me. They heat the blanket in a microwave then cover the patient with it. It is one of the most comforting and delicious sensations that I have ever had. That is what I felt like when that "blanket" called bankruptcy came down over me.

So again I ask, why not bankruptcy? Yes I know there is a downside but that so pales compared to the upside. Remember, it is moot to worry about how a bankruptcy will affect your credit report, your report is already probably in the toilet. In reality, a bankruptcy is one of the best ways to build up your credit.

Why bankruptcy over debt management, debt settlement and debt consolidation? Their programs are based upon what they need, not what you need and what you can afford to pay. Their programs will no doubt include budget busting payments. You will pay handsomely for the "privilege" of them taking this whole sordid mess off your hands. These companies are powerful forces staffed by some of the best salespeople in the world, you are no match for them.

You will find these players the most violently vocal about how bad bankruptcy is and boy are you lucky you talked to them first. They have a strong motivation to talk you out of bankruptcy and that is to make a lot of money at your expense. They benefit from your debt problem while making your problem worse, not better. Every time someone opts for bankruptcy it means a loss of revenue for them. With bankruptcy there is no need for a management, settlement or consolidation company to "work with you".

If not for the unmitigated greed of the credit card companies, there would be far less need for bankruptcy. The relationship between the creditor and the debtor would be more of a symbiotic relationship. Consumers receive a service and they need to pay for that service in the form of interest. But when the interest jumps at the whim of the company to loan shark status, there goes that symbiotic relationship. We then have a slave/master relationship and no good can come of that.

You are now in a toxic relationship, one that bears you no good will. Bankruptcy is the antidote. There are many reasons for you to opt out of this debt nightmare. It is not even the case of bankruptcy being the lesser of the two evils, that of being stuck on "debt row hell" or getting a second chance, a fresh slate. How many times in life do we actually get to do that?

Many debtors may hesitate to file for bankruptcy because they have no money for an attorney. Do not let that stop you. Many attorneys will give you a free consultation and advise you on the best course of action for your particular case. If you are still throwing money at creditors, stop and put it towards your bankruptcy.

In the case of the Chapter 13 bankruptcy, the lion's share of the attorney's fee, about 90 percent, is paid out of the payments made to the trustee. Whatever an attorney does charge you is a fraction of what you probably owe, and is money well spent.

A debtor may feel that bankruptcy is way too complicated and stressful. Uh excuse me, aren't you under an unbelievable burden of stress already over your financial situation? After you get your paperwork filled out, there is no work on your part, your attorney does all the work.

The magical day will finally arrive when this documentation is submitted to the bankruptcy court. You will know that day, that is the day the phone stops ringing with collection calls. It is the day you can go to your mailbox and not hold your breath, hoping you will not find another nasty summons. It is the first day of the rest of your life, the life you just took back with your bankruptcy.

Within about 60 days you will receive from your regional bankruptcy court a date to appear before the bankruptcy trustee. This meeting is known as the meeting of the creditors, the 341 meeting, a meeting creditors hardly ever show up for. You need not worry about having to face your creditors, chances are excellent they won't show up.

When you receive the notice to appear, you may start worrying about what will happen in court. Don't. I was fully prepared to give a full fledged explanation of how we found ourselves in bankruptcy court. This was not like going to municipal court for a housing code violation. The worst that could have happened to us there was to be put in jail. I was afraid if the bankruptcy trustee did not think we had a "good" enough reason to be seeking protection from creditors, we would not get a confirmation. That would mean we would be back on our own, fending off the wolves again. That was a gruesome thought. All of my worrying was just a waste of time though. They never even asked why or how it happened. It did not matter a bit to them, which was fine by me. We were just another couple in a long line of couples that day.

While it does not matter to the court why you got into a debt crisis, it needs to matter to you. If you do not understand how you got where you did, how will you ever address the problem so it will not re-occur? That understanding holds the key to your post bankruptcy prosperity.

After you and your attorney have your first, and sometimes your only, meeting with the bankruptcy trustee, one of two things will happen. Your case can be confirmed the same day by the bankruptcy judge or your confirmation can be delayed up until a future date to work out any revisions in the repayment plan. In our case there were two amendments to our plan. One was that it would be for 60 months instead of the proposed 51 and that any tax refunds we receive during the 60 months was to go into the plan. Our attorney went back to the court two months later for the confirmation of the amended plan, we did not even have to go. It was confirmed and it was over. As long as we pay our monthly payment, we receive our discharge in 60 months.

After what we had been through, we could do this standing on our head.

I don't care that we have a bankruptcy on our credit report. Judgments and liens on our credit report would have been worse. We would never have been free from the crushing and debilitating yoke of debt were it not for bankruptcy. We were saved in every sense of the word.

If your debt is manageable and you can pay it off without hardship to you or your family, pay it off. If you can without depriving yourself and your family of basic necessities and essentials, then you should. Sacrificing your retirement, your children's education, health expenses, mortgage, food, utilities, to throw money at debt that will take you years and years, if ever, to pay off, is most certainly not the best solution for you and your family. Yes, you may feel you have an obligation to pay off your debts, after all you did sign up for them right? However you did not sign up to be raked over the coals by the credit card companies, just because they can.

Sometimes we just think that "giving up" is not an option. Throwing up our hands and saying "you got me" is not a palatable idea to us. We think we will just eat hamburger helper and live in a hovel for the rest of our lives if we have to but we are going to pay that debt back if it kills us. Maybe it won't kill you but your life will most likely look like one most would not envy.

When you have fought the good fight and lost, do you know when to stop and save yourself? I had always wanted to learn how to scuba dive. I loved to snorkel and thought if I learned to scuba dive, there would be so much more to see and so I signed up for lessons. The book instruction was easy but when it came to the actual scuba diving part, that was another story. We had to practice in the pool with full scuba gear on. Anyone who has ever had scuba gear on knows how cumbersome it is. Yes I know, once you are in the water it is supposed to be manageable, not in my case however. Somehow it had escaped my notice that one needed to have at least some semblance of co-ordination to scuba dive. I had none. I am the original "can't walk and chew gum" at the same time type of gal. Once suited up and in the water, I had no control over my body. It was just going every which way. When we had to venture out into the deep water, I was petrified, poised at the drop off. Having no control was the terror, I just knew once the side of the pool was not available for me to grab onto, I was going to be a goner. The instructor kept beckoning me to come out to the deep water while I just kept shaking my head no. Finally he had to come and get me and prop me up through the scuba exercises.

After the session he said as diplomatically as possible that he did not think I was anywhere near ready for the open water certification that was coming up. The open water certification is when they take you out to a lake or quarry and you have to pass different ability tests in order to be certified. This was the real thing. I assured him that I was going to practice everyday and conquer my fear and control my co-ordination.

Every day for the next two weeks you could find me at my sister's pool, practicing for the open water certification. When I would try and go through the exercises I would keep flipping over and getting stuck, like a turtle on its' back. Through sheer stubbornness I was able to execute the certification requirements. Of course I was only in 4 feet of water.

The day of the certification arrived and on the drive to the quarry where it would be held I was full of confidence. We all suited up and entered the quarry. The instructor was my dive buddy. We were down about a whole 8 feet when I panicked and wildly gestured up, up to the instructor. He got me to the top and towed me into shore. As I slunk out of the water, past little kids happily diving in with not a trace of fear, dragging my sorry self over to a picnic table, I collapsed onto it in a dripping heap.

I didn't try to shed any of my gear, I was too weak from defeat to move. All I could do was sit there and try to decide whether to give it up or continue to risk it all to prove to myself I could. How bad did I want to see the pretty fishes, enough to kill myself? When you are scuba diving you need to do several different functions at the same time, failure to do so could result in your death or worse, ending up in a coma or brain dead.

By the time I dragged myself, still in full scuba gear, off that picnic table, I knew the answer. This sure was not worth dying for. The instructor walked up to me and told me I needed more pool time. I told him all the pool time in the world was not going to remove my fear. I thanked him for his patience and hard work but I knew when to quit. Do you know when to quit and save yourself, to live another day, a life worth living?

It just might be that day you decide to file bankruptcy and seek protection from the legal system from your creditors. The day we did I was reminded of my scuba debacle. It is of course admirable when we try to pay our debts but we must know, for our own good, when to give up the good fight. When we know we tried our very best and that still was not good enough, it is time to save ourselves. Being stubborn and determined to see this thing through if it kills you, well just may kill you. We do not need to go through life with the anchor of unresolved debt around our neck, dragging us down, precluding any chance we may have for a future worth living, constantly looking over our shoulder.

The majority of bankruptcies filed are Chapter 7. They are shorter, cheaper and will wipe out all unsecured debt. There is no limit to the debt that can be discharged, it can be in the millions. This debt is usually in the form of credit card debt, medical bills and personal loans. A means test is applied to those seeking a Chapter 7. Those making $100,000 or less will have no trouble qualifying. They do nothing for loans like mortgages, child support, taxes and student loans. However, there are some exceptions to the student loan debt. You pay nothing back but your assets may be liquidated. However often you get to keep your home, depending on how much equity you have. Typically a Chapter 7 takes about 4 to 6 months to wind its way through the court and then it is discharged. Typically lenders make you wait two years after your discharge to apply for a mortgage. However with the multitudes of people seeking bankruptcy protection, that waiting period could even be shortened in the future. The powers that be change the rules all the time to fit their agenda.

Far less file for Chapter 13. People who wish to hold onto their property, as we did, would find this the best option for them. It is more complex, expensive and lasts much longer, from 3 to 5 years. There is a limit of debt for a Chapter 13. You may have no more than one million in secured debt and $350,000 in unsecured debt. The amount you must repay has no bearing on what you owe in debts. It is determined by what you have left over after your expenses are met for the month. Typically the bankruptcy court will request your tax returns every year. If your situation changes, for instance if you get a better job and have more income, they may raise your monthly payments.

Before you meet with an attorney to discuss bankruptcy, amend your W-2 to reflect the highest number of deductions possible. Why? Because they can mandate that any tax refund go directly to the plan, meaning you don't get it. You do not want a return since you can't keep it anyway. You want that extra money every month in your paycheck.

You can get a mortgage and a car loan while in a Chapter 13 as long as it is approved by the trustee. You can also get refinancing on your home.

Chapter 13 costs from $2000 to $4000, but remember the majority of this fee comes out of the payments you make to the trustee. You may think you are too broke to even retain an attorney. Find a way. If you were dying and needed that money to pay for some wonder drug to save your life, you would find it. Well you are dying, our financial life is so intertwined with our natural life, sometimes they seem to be indistinguishable.

If you are still sending money every month to the credit card companies or a debt management/settlement/consolidation plan, give that money instead to a bankruptcy attorney. It will be the best money you ever spent, with the biggest return. And for a change, that money will make a difference in your life, a big one. After years of sending money to that black hole, with seemingly no end in sight, immediately you see the light.

"I feel like I got a really good deal on a used car" says Mary Kay Place to Kevin Klein in the movie "*The Big Chill*" as he consents to "donate" his sperm to impregnate her as her biological clock is going off. That is how it felt. Not only did we get those pesky collectors and summons to stop, we got to keep everything, our home, apartments, cars, rental house and pension. Chances are excellent you will get to keep all or most of your assets in a Chapter 13. All states have different exemptions as to what is protected in a bankruptcy.

I would hope this is unnecessary warning but you must cease and desist using credit cards. You cannot hope to reverse this situation by adding to it. Incurring more debt is not the answer to prospering. Bankruptcy courts will surely take notice if you went on a spending spree and ran up debt right before filing. That will not bode well for your petition. With the salvation of bankruptcy at your fingertips, why would anyone do anything so foolish as to jeopardize it? Besides, if you hope to prosper after your bankruptcy you better get used to learning to live without plastic. Yes it may be an adjustment, maybe even a painful one but nowhere near the pain of drowning in debt. You can never hope to prosper if you continue to pay two to three times more for everything you consume and continue to risk your future. We have not had a credit card in many years and the freedom is beyond mere words. Imagine going to the mailbox and never finding a bill from the credit card companies. How great it is knowing we will never again have to pay in the future for what we consumed in the past.

With a bankruptcy you know your "spring" date, the date you are done for good, unlike the lingering uncertainty of bad debt chasing you around for the rest of your natural born life. You get absolution and resolution at the same time. Life is good again.

You may hear critics warning that a bankruptcy stays on your credit report for 7 to 10 years. My response would be "so?". That notation on my credit report hurts me far less that the pain suffered on "debt row hell". If having a bankruptcy recorded on my credit report is the price to pay for freedom, I will gladly pay it.

If you hope to prosper after your bankruptcy you should be looking at credit only for large purchases like a house and a car. This book is not just about surviving bankruptcy, it is also about prospering. You want to prosper, you know what the view is like at the bottom, not so pretty.

You may fear everyone will know if you file for bankruptcy. Unless you are a famous person it is highly unlikely anyone else would have to know.

If you are paying on a mortgage loan or any other loan not included in the bankruptcy you just keep paying directly to them, your payments are not funneled through the court.

It is a huge misconception that only deadbeats file for bankruptcy. The myth has unduly kept many from saving themselves. It is people just like you and me. It could be because of a life altering situation like death, divorce, illness or loss of income. It could just as easily be because so many depend on credit to meet everyday, basic needs. It could be to fund an entrepreneurial venture, as it was with us. It is also due to the fact that many live far above their means and cannot get out of that cycle. Many times it is a combination of all or some of the above, by people who find themselves in the position where their debt grows instead of shrinks, even as they struggle to pay it. Most who file have struggled for years on end to try and keep up, but the game is rigged and not in our favor.

If you are struggling to make your credit card payments at the expense of your basic human necessities like food, shelter and utilities, it may be time to talk to a good bankruptcy attorney. The more dischargeable debts you have like credit card debt, signature loans and medical bills, the more reason you have to choose bankruptcy as the very best possible situation for you and your family.

The longer you put it off the more you will spend in money and pain. In my research that was a common thread in people who filed bankruptcy, they only wished they had done it sooner.

If your debt is rising to meet your income, you are in serious trouble. When you are paying out everything, or close to everything, to your creditors, how will you live? You will then basically be living and working strictly to pay off your creditors. Before you know it you will turn around and realize you worked your whole life for your creditors. What a pity. There was a song popular in the 60's called "Sixteen Tons". It was about a coal miner and how his whole life was intertwined with the coal company. The coal company paid the miners salary, they in turn spent all their money on company owned housing and stores. One line in the song was "St. Peter, don't call me cause I can't go, I owe my soul to the company store". But that does not have to be your fate.

For all the people that use credit card debt to survive, there are some who abuse credit cards because, well because they can. They can get more stuff and get it now. Many are simply conspicuous consumers or at least ravenous consumers and the advent of easy credit has made it so easy to indulge their proclivity for spending for the sake of spending, consumerism for the sheer gratification of it all. Bankruptcy alone is not going to cure that.

Bankruptcy is not the end of your financial life. Rather it can be the beginning of more prosperity than you could have imagined when you were drowning in debt.

Bankruptcy is not the scarlet letter it used to be. The sentiment has shifted. Logic would prevail that sometimes a bankruptcy is the very best option. The benefits of a bankruptcy are so obvious that many debtors who struggle and do without to repay their debt are considered more foolish than noble. The pendulum has swung wide since the middle ages.

Bankruptcy gives you your life back. It is impossible to live up to our full potential when every waking thought is consumed with thoughts of how to pay unmanageable debt. When you have your life back, you get to make plans again. Remember making plans?

CHAPTER ELEVEN

HOW TO PROSPER AFTER BANKRUPTCY

No, this chapter is not going to be about get rich schemes. In order to achieve prosperity you must understand that there is no such thing as a get rich quick scheme, however there is a get rich slowly scheme.

The sad truth is that people who are enamored of the get rich school of thought are really handicapping their hope for true and lasting prosperity. Many people will spend their whole life chasing one get rich scheme after another, only to find themselves at the end of life with nothing. The real tragedy is that if they had instead set about to get rich slowly, they would have ended up with all the prosperity they needed with no worries about how they would be spending the rest of their life.

Why do get rich schemes fail? Think of gambling. You can gamble and lose so of course you gamble some more until eventually you win. But then what? It goes right back into the slot machine or to the convenience store clerk until eventually you lose it all again. There are some gamblers that will take their winnings and quit while ahead but they are in the minority, most will gamble every last dollar back.

Just flip through the channels on a weekend or late at night and you will find plenty of infomercials promising that if you buy their material you will find yourself swimming in money. I often wondered if the ideas were that good why were they wasting their time trying to sell the idea, why weren't they out doing it themselves and making all that money they claim you can make. The truth is there is great wealth in these products, for the individuals selling them, not the people watching and eventually whipping out the credit card and buying the program.

Television is awash with infomercials proclaiming how easy it is to get rich in real estate. Would-be get rich quick real estate investors watch these programs, more often than not actually buying the product. They may go so far as to read and listen to the materials. Some will try to employ the techniques taught. But it is not easy, simple in premise yes, but not in execution. The materials then get set on the top shelf of the closet or maybe end up at the garage sale, so ending another's dream of easy riches.

All get rich quick schemes have the same thread running through it. The scheme is selling the fantasy that it is easy to get rich in a hurry. That is what they sell and that is what the consumer buys, the illusion. Chase illusion long enough and you will have squandered whatever time and resources you have on this earth.

You have been given a fantastic opportunity to turn your life around, to go from the pit of financial despair to being financially secure. Unimaginable wealth is also a very real possibility. When struggling in survival mode, the thought of wealth was probably the last thought on your mind.

Wealth is a relative word, what is wealth to one would not be to another. You alone get to decide just how much wealth you will want to have to sustain a lifestyle of your choice.

The opportunity you have been given are the fruits of your ordeal with your life before bankruptcy, when you were on a treadmill, sprinting away but going nowhere, actually you were probably going backwards. But thanks to the magic of bankruptcy, you get the slate wiped clean. You have been given a gift, put it to very good use. Now you can start going forward. You now have a future, you won't continue to squander it. Now that you have your future back, make good use of it. Learn to pay it forward, not pay it back.

Bankruptcy won't catapult you to prosperity. But it can open whole new realms of possibilities for you to prosper to a degree you probably never thought possible.

You must know by now that credit cards are counterproductive to achieving prosperity. You must swear off credit cards for life. You cannot expect to prosper if you keep returning to debt, if you do you have learned nothing. You will start receiving credit card offers almost immediately. Shred the applications. If you are sent a pre-approved card, contact the issuer and tell them you don't want it. If you don't contact the issuer, it will show up on your credit report as open credit. NO CREDIT CARDS.

While doing research for this book, the one question that was asked repeatedly by people going through a bankruptcy was how soon could they get another credit card. What? Why would anyone who has struggled with credit card debt and been lucky enough to get a second chance, want to again start using credit cards? That is incredulous, not to mention stupid.

Don't believe the myth you need a credit card to book a hotel room, rent a car, travel or order online. I have done all that with a debit card. I have traveled in Europe, Mexico and Canada with no more than a debit card. Remember to alert your bank that you will be out of the country, just as you would with a credit card. Don't delude yourself into thinking you need just one. You don't.

You may think you need a credit card for emergencies, that you need that security. You just know the car will break down or the stove will go and then what will you do? It is a fact of life there will always be some sort of emergency. Remember all that money you sent every month to the credit card companies? Instead save that very same money, before you know it you will have the money you need for that emergency and you won't need a credit card. Think of having a credit card as having a loaded gun in the house for protection. It is far more likely that the gun will be used to your harm than to your good.

A great couch on sale is not an emergency. If you really want that couch a far better plan would be to save for it, now there is a novel idea, one that hasn't been too popular for quite a while. Now would be as good a time as ever to start practicing that unique concept again, after all, we are starting over. We are perfectly positioned for prosperity to come our way.

Whether you are 22 or 92, think for a minute of all the money you have made thus far in your life. The older you are the more money you have had time to make. Now think of where it all went. Do you know? That's a sobering thought. "On living" you might think first. Yes, living takes a chunk out of the money we make throughout our lives. But if you are honest, you know there are huge amounts that we cannot account for if our lives depended on it. We probably have all frittered away fortunes. That hurts. But it is a new day, remember fresh slate and all. It is time to show your money who the boss is. If you do not know where your money is going, you won't know where it went, your money would be MIA. When you don't know where your money went, you lose control and if you lose control how can you expect to prosper?

I offer you a very basic concept about money. If we spend $1.00 on one thing, we do not have it to spend on another thing. Remember, time is far more precious than money. Do you ever think that you trade precious hours of your life for money? This is what we do to survive. We go to work to earn a paycheck to sustain ourselves and our family. We are OK with this, we know we have to work to live, unless you are one of the unfortunate people who were born wealthy and never had to worry about money. Yes, you read that right, I did say unfortunate. Look at all you miss. If you never had to work or strive for something, how boring and empty life would be. You would never know the joy of accomplishment, of doing something on your own. If you had everything handed to you, life would be a constant quest for meaning.

While we work for the necessities in life, food, shelter and utilities, we also spend a lot of time working for our wants and desires, for what is life if it is to be austere, if all we are doing is surviving. The secret is to realize the true cost of what you are trading for what you are getting. You want to buy a coat for $200. You make $18.00 an hour. How many hours would you have to work, to take out of your life, to pay for the coat? You would have to work 11 hours and 11 minutes. Yes but you love that coat and are prepared to give up 11 hours and 11 minutes of your life for it. That's fine, that's your prerogative, mankind's free will at its' best. But wait, you may decide that coat is not worth 11 hours and 11 minutes of your time, maybe the color isn't exactly right. At least you took the time to analyze and make an informed decision about buying the coat.

Don't stop at the coat, that is how you should view all discretionary spending. You will be pleasantly surprised how fast your money will grow once you do. When you realize what you trade your precious hours for, you will be a lot more discriminating.

When I worked a 9-5 job I was able to take my vacation in hour increments. Checking the Nazi time clock everyday, I would gleefully add up my stockpile of precious vacation hours. In the summer I would combine my lunch hour with 3 hours of vacation and take the afternoon off to enjoy the sun. Wiling away the summer day, I had this mental picture of an hourglass, with the tiny beads of sand slipping through. I hoarded my vacation hours so I could enjoy my free time but lamented how fast they slipped away. That is how fast your money can slip away if you do not realize the precious price you pay, in work hours, for everything you spend money on.

Am I suggesting you live a poor austere life? Not at all, I don't. I am suggesting that you be aware of every bit of money you spend and you will spend a lot less when you think of what you are giving up.

You need to honestly analyze how you got into the financial situation that resulted in your bankruptcy. You must be brutally honest with yourself. If you do not know how you got into that situation how do you hope to avoid it in the future? How do you expect to prosper if you have not learned from your bankruptcy? You can't. So dig down and figure out exactly why. Sometimes it's a combination of factors. This can be one of life's greatest and most beneficial learning experience, so take advantage of it.

Factors like divorce, job loss and a health crisis are all unavoidable and sometimes unforeseen forces which you may have little control over. There are also factors that you have some control over, such as cost of living. Then there are factors that you have total control over, like living above your means, "keeping up with the Jones" (that is so over) and wanting it all, right now. You, and I, do not have to impress the Jones, we only have to impress ourselves.

We live in an age of instant gratification. We want it all and we want it now. So we buy on credit and doom ourselves to a perpetual cycle of debt, like a hamster on a wheel. That's us, running, running, and going around in a circle, never going anywhere. I have no desire to back on that wheel and would hope you don't either.

Learn the art of delayed gratification, it is so much more rewarding than instant. Now that you are no longer saddled with the monthly yoke of credit card payments, you now get to keep that very same money you were slavishly sending every month. Now you have the money to pay for things you would have nonchalantly put on credit. You will appreciate something much more when you pay for it and know you truly own it. As you won't be paying twice as much for it, you will be able to afford twice as much. I really like that part. You are becoming prosperous.

If you want to become prosperous you need to pay yourself first. I know you have heard this old chestnut ad nauseum many times, but it works. You sit down to pay your bills every month, wouldn't it be fun to get a check from yourself? You worked for it, you pay the mortgage, utilities, insurance premiums so where is your cut? Didn't you earn it? Even if you start out with a paltry sum, that's OK. It's the habit you are trying to get into not so much the amount. It is behavior modification and it works. Once you make something a habit, it is hard to break. I like the envelope system, once it goes into the envelope, that piece of paper might as well be Fort Knox for I do not go back into it unless it is to add more or to retrieve it for the purpose it was intended.

Know your net worth. If you have never done a net worth statement, do it now. For those who have already had a bankruptcy, they will find that their net worth has gone up. Doing a net worth statement is easy. Add up all your assets, cash, all sources of income (pay, rents, royalties) investments, real estate owned, (appraised value) auto (value), retirement accounts/pensions and any other assets you own. Then list all your liabilities (what you owe), mortgages, installment loans, credit card debt (of which should be zero after a bankruptcy). If you are in a Chapter 13, you would include that payment. You then subtract your liabilities from your assets and that is your net worth.

While you are planning for your prosperous future, you need to know where you are up to this point. That is what your net worth tells you. Your net worth is the sum total of your past financial decisions. Once you have that figure, your net worth, you can better plan on how to increase that number.

If you are pre-bankruptcy as you read this, you will see how credit card debt has eaten into your net worth. It is usually the case that these purchases have no value, they are not assets, they are liabilities, plain and simple. If you are lucky enough to be reading this post bankruptcy, you will see how the absence of credit card debt has increased your net worth. Let's keep it that way. Our mission now is to increase our net worth, we already have a huge head start with the erasing of the credit card debt. Let us show our appreciation and prosper!

There is a six letter word that we all hate. Budget. I am not going to talk about a budget. Let's call it something else. A blueprint, a map to prosperity or how about a game plan. Budget sounds like some sort of deprivation and we don't like it. Let's instead use a positive word for this instrument. Remember the vast amounts of money we have probably made and spent in our lifetimes and we probably cannot pinpoint with any accuracy where it all went, except to say "on living".

The more control you have over your money, the more money you will have, and keep. If you have gone through a Chapter 13, you had to do an income and expense statement. All your income minus all your expenses. Whatever was left over was what you paid into your repayment plan, as long as they accepted it. That may have been the first time you actually put down on paper what your expenses were. In order for the prosperity benefit of a bankruptcy to be realized, you must, whether you like it or not, get your expenses down on paper. You may not realize how much you have been spending, or maybe overspending, in your life. Not knowing is like driving with a blindfold, you just hope you don't run off the road. Not good enough!

If you have been through a bankruptcy this is a piece of cake. Now, thanks to your debts being erased, or greatly reduced in the case of a Chapter 13, you should be pleasantly surprised at what you now have to work with. This is your big chance, your golden opportunity to be on your way to prosperity. Not only should you have more to work with, you should have discovered how much less you can actually live on, like you did when you had no choice. When you had no money and your cards were maxed out to where you couldn't even use them, you learned how to get by on a lot less. Chances are excellent you too engaged in some couch diving for change.

Now that your debts have been legally wiped out, or you are paying back a paltry sum in a Chapter 13, it is time to see how high you can soar. What will you do with the money you have now that you had previously been slavishly sending to the credit card companies? Glad you asked.

We know there is good debt and bad debt. Credit card debt is bad debt, very bad debt. Good debt would be mortgage debt for your home and investment property. While we certainly don't need credit card debt, we usually need mortgage debt. Very few people can pay cash for a house. It is a myth that you need to establish credit to get a mortgage. What you do need is steady income and a down payment. Too many people think they need credit card debt to establish credit so they can buy a house. But more often than not, that plan backfires. Even if they have not been late on payments or have no defaults, a debt load is taken into consideration by the bank when you apply for a loan. If you are carrying too much credit debt you may not qualify for a loan, it is called debt to income ratio. If the ratios between your debt and your income are not within the underwriting guidelines, no house for you.

Instead of getting a house you instead get a load of crippling debt. By the same token if you are hoping to buy a house, do not go out and buy a car with a huge monthly payment. As a realtor I had many clients who wanted to buy a house but when they applied for a loan their car payment ballooned their debt to income ratio and they could not get a loan for a house. Hope they liked the car, they may have to live in it. An expensive vehicle is certainly not on the super highway to prosperity. We have bought houses for less than some people pay for their vehicles.

For those of you who already have a home and most likely a mortgage, you have a perfect way to greatly accelerate your net worth. What will you do with the money that you used to throw down that black hole every month? How about paying off your mortgage years early? The money you save in interest alone would probably be enough to buy a vacation condo. Remember the hundreds of dollars you were sending every month to Chase, Discover and American Express? If you applied even some of that money every month towards your principal you would be on a fast track to prosperity. You had to send it to the creditors every month, making them richer, now use that same money to make you richer.

You don't even have to discipline yourself to do it, you've already been doing it, for someone's else's benefit. How hard would it be to do it for your own benefit? And such a benefit it is, a paid off house years earlier than expected. What will you do once you don't have to make house payments? I can think of a few things. You will have a paid off house and saved thousands upon thousands of dollars. There are few things in life that gives a greater sense of security than having a paid off house.

Obviously the more extra you pay every month on the principal, the faster you will pay it off and the more money you will save. But just making one extra principal payment a year can knock off 7 years on a 30 year loan. If you are on year 10 of a 30 year loan and you make one extra payment a year, instead of having 20 years to go, you only have 13. Just think how much sooner you would pay it off if you made 2 extra payments. That would be a fabulous use for a tax refund check. If making 1 or 2 extra payments a year seems like too much, you can instead make the equivalent of that extra pay or two every month.

Example, your mortgage payment is $1200 a month. If you paid an extra $100 a month, paying $1300 instead of $1200, that would accomplish the same goal. At the end of the year that extra $100 adds up to $1200, or an extra month's payment. An extra $100 a month, $25 a week or $3.57 a day. Can you find an extra $3.57 a day? If you want to make 2 extra payments a year, add $200, paying $1400 a month. Can you squeeze out an extra $7.14 a day? Whatever sacrifices you make to pay extra on your mortgage will increase your wealth exponentially.

There is also the bi-weekly mortgage where you pay your mortgage every two weeks instead of once a month with the result being you make 13 payments a year instead of 12. There are 12 months in a year and 52 weeks. Paying every 2 weeks would result in 13 payments instead of 12. Lenders and escrow companies will be happy to set up your mortgage on this schedule for you but they will of course be charging you a fee to do so.

If you want to calculate the savings you would reap by making just one extra payment a year, go to www.mortgage-x.com. Remember if your taxes and insurance are escrowed in with your principal and interest, your home payoff is accelerated even more, as the extra money is all going directly to the principal. Make sure that the extra mortgage money is in fact going on the principal. Check your statements diligently. Usually your statement will have a space on it to denote if you are paying extra on the principal. If it does not, then you be sure and note it on the statement you send in with your payment. Be very diligent about tracking your extra payments, don't assume someone at the other end is doing their job. Save every statement that records the extra principal payments you are making. You always want to have proof you made the payments.

There is another method to accelerate your mortgage payoff. You can pay off a mortgage in half the time. If you have 20 years to go on a 30 year mortgage, you can pay it off in 10 years. Whatever time you have left, lop off half. This method will cost you a bit more each month though. When you pay your mortgage payment for the month, include an additional principal only payment. In the beginning of a loan, the principal is usually very small and the interest is very high. As the years go by, the balance shifts, the portion going to principal goes up and the portion going to interest goes down. If you are in the first few years of a mortgage, the principal payments will be less, as the years go by the extra amount will increase.

I would add that conventional wisdom dictates that while your mortgage payment is growing every month because the principal portion grows as the interest portion shrinks, your income usually grows too. Even if you could only do this for a few years think of how much further ahead you would be financially.

The financial gurus and pundits will tell you to invest that money in the markets instead, especially if you have a low interest rate. Of course as we all know now so painfully, that is not guaranteed money. When you pay your mortgage down, that is guaranteed money. Think of the money you save in interest by paying down your loan faster. Then think of how long it would take you to actually go out and EARN that same money. You are doing no extra work by paying down your mortgage. Now that is what I call easy money. Most important, think how secure you will feel with a paid off house.

Try this. Call the institution that holds your mortgage and ask for a loan modification. A modification is not a refinance, a loan modification just modifies the terms of the loan you already have with the lender. A friend who has a mortgage with the same lender as we do told me that he got a loan modification and I should try and get one too. I was skeptical. Surely they would not modify our loan while we were in a bankruptcy. I took a chance and called the bank and asked for one. Within two days we were sitting in front of the loan officer modifying our loan for a full 1% lower interest rate. I held my breath until the final papers were signed, about two weeks later. I was sure that at any given moment they would call and say, "Oh so sorry, we made a mistake, you have a bankruptcy, we cannot modify your loan". But they didn't and two weeks later we signed the papers and turbo-charged our ride to prosperity. The extra money saved every month is going directly onto the principal. Call your lender and ask, if you don't ask, you don't get.

When it comes to reaping prosperity in life, we can be our own biggest stumbling block. The problem for many of us is that we are so busy worrying about our finances today, we cannot even think honestly about 5, 10 or 29 years down the road. Well here is a cheery thought, the only alternative is your premature demise. That's no solution. Short of shuffling off this mortal coil, we will all arrive years down the road, and I would just as soon arrive prosperous.

With prosperity comes freedom, freedom to do whatever you want, whenever your want. Freedom is one of the most precious commodities we can ever hope to achieve in this lifetime. Many wars have been fought and too many lives have been lost all for the sake of freedom. You know what it is like to be shackled and enslaved in debt, that makes the freedom you will enjoy all the sweeter. We have experienced the lows of credit card debt nightmare, now it is time to experience the highs of financial freedom.

It is no small surprise that people fail to plan for the future. Since we live in an instant gratification world, we want it all and we want it all right now. We think we will never get any older, we are modern day Peter Pans. While we are all sure we want a wonderful retirement, we are too busy paying for today to actually apply the principles that will make that dream come true. One day I was standing in line at the bank. A young man in his 20's was asking about various savings programs offered by the bank. The teller proceeded to tell him about a wonderful program they had for retirement. "Oh, no, no, I am not interested in that, that is too far off for me to even think of", the young man replied. While I was standing there eavesdropping, I couldn't help but think that if that young man only realized how lucky he was, to be young enough to actually start stockpiling a fortune. Too often people can't think that far down the road, that far down the road doesn't exist for them. Even if they were concerned about the future, they are too busy just trying to get through the present.

It does not matter what age you are, there is still time to achieve prosperity. Thanks to your bankruptcy, you are perfectly positioned to do just that. The adversity you experienced will work in your favor on your road to prosperity. Look, you already know how resourceful and resilient you can be, you are a bankruptcy survivor. You either got all or the majority of your debts wiped out in bankruptcy court. That should translate into your having some disposable income you can apply towards your future prosperity. For all those times when you scraped together the minimum payment to send to your creditor, can you not find the extra money now to put towards your wealth?

Over the long haul, the markets have always performed. If you don't have a lot of time to ride a market out this is probably not the best bet for you. If you have a lot of years on hand, think young guy in bank, you certainly can gain wealth by investing. The money you have been sending to creditors every month could now go instead to investing for your future. When your Chapter 13 plan was confirmed, you had to account for all of your money. They may take notice that you have money for investing and think instead it should go into your repayment plan. I would check with my lawyer on that one.

Here's a fun tip for you. Would you like to save thousands of dollars a year on consumer goods? Two words, garage sales. I have bought furniture, home furnishings, electronic equipment, clothes, toys, gifts, tools, books, and DVD's, for pennies on the dollar. I bought $50 shirts with tags still on them for $2, a 3 piece glass and steel table set for $20 and a new pair of $100 boots, brand new, still in the box for $25. The best deal I got was a 9 year old $5000 swimming pool, loaded, for $300. Besides saving thousands of dollars a year, it is fun. It satisfies our inherent need to acquire for next to nothing practically. How much better can it get! The trick is to go to the better neighborhoods, this is where you find the best loot. Not only can you find practical and useful items but you have a very good chance of finding some treasure you never knew you always wanted. Try it, let me warn you though, it is addictive.

Remember above all else, while we want to prosper financially to insure our independence and freedom, never lose sight of the fact that the greatest prosperity cannot be measured in dollars. Never forget that we can always make money but we cannot make more time. We are all allotted so much time and we must embrace every minute. While we need to plan for the future, remember to live in the moment. Money is endless, time is not. At least once a day, stop and reflect on the very moment you are in. Enjoy that moment, even if you are stuck in traffic or doing your least favorite chore. Embrace your loved ones and yourself, cherish every moment of their life and yours. Know that with a bankruptcy, you have survived a crisis that has only served to make you stronger, wiser and wealthier.

CHAPTER TWELVE

GETTING YOUR LIFE AND FUTURE BACK

Do you want to know what one of life's best kept secrets is? It is bankruptcy. At first blush, it may seem like a failure, something nobody would wish to have happen in their life. But it is not. If you had the chance to put this craziness behind you why wouldn't you? You have already gone through the pain and despair that led up to this crisis. Filing bankruptcy is when the healing begins. It is when you will finally get closure to a problem you thought would follow you for the rest of your life.

Understand the fragility of life. A financial burden that you cannot carry will devastate your life as quickly and as surely as an illness or an accident.

I so needed closure. Going through the rest of my life looking over my shoulder, always waiting for the other shoe to drop was not a life worth looking forward to. It was a certainty to me that just when I thought they had forgotten about us, wham, some debt collector chases us down and slaps a lawsuit on us. What kind of way is that to go through life? That cloud hovering right over your head will color and dictate many actions you take, or fail to take, in life.

When going through a severe financial crisis you come to believe you have no life, that life is a mere memory. And as for a future, you think "what future?"

I wanted to move on and get my life back. I wanted not to fear every time the phone or doorbell rang. I wanted not to hide behind the curtain or in the basement or drag my steps to the mailbox everyday worrying who was suing us today. I wanted not to pass up my driveway when coming home and finding a strange car in the driveway and a person who looked suspiciously like a process server lurking around the house. I wanted to feel like I was not a hardened criminal who committed a grievous act and was deserving of the hell that had become my life. Most of all I wanted absolution, I wanted to know this financial disaster was not fatal, it was in fact forgivable, in every sense of the word.

Receiving absolution through the legal system is about as good as it gets. Your salvation is sanctioned by the law. It's nice to have the law on your side. After being beat up and beat down by creditors and collectors for so long, you can finally put that all behind you and start to live again.

Many fear a bankruptcy because of what it will do to their credit score. This is not the time to be worrying about your score, accept that it is trashed. A bankruptcy can only help it, eventually. Charge-offs, collections, liens and judgments are no better and they don't go away, at least not until they are paid, if ever. With a bankruptcy, you will probably know to the day when you are free of that baggage.

Maybe you need to feel that you have tried your hardest and exhausted every possible way you can think of to pay down your debt rather than to file bankruptcy. Only you know when you are at that point when you have done all you can do and can do no more.

If you see no way out of this hole, if collectors have you on speed dial, when you realize you are sacrificing your future for your past, when you struggle every month to make payments only to see your debt grow or at best shrink at a snail's pace, you may be ready. If you see yourself in your golden years bagging groceries at the market or living with your kids, you may be ready. When you are sick and tired of being sick and tired of laying awake at night trying to figure out how you are going to scrape together the money needed to keep your creditors at bay, you may be ready.

The longer you put off filing the more money and emotion you will have wasted. When you are struggling with the debilitating effects of excessive debt, you are on a downward spiral. Depression and despair haunts you, it becomes your new best friend, it invites itself into your life and takes up residence. It is hard to think logically and make good decisions when you are scared.

Bankruptcy will give you a second chance and you deserve that. The question is, what will you do with your second chance?

www.ingramcontent.com/pod-product-compliance
Lightning Source LLC
Chambersburg PA
CBHW051534170526
45165CB00002B/723